The Atheist's Tragedy

CYRIL TOURNEUR

Edited by
BRIAN MORRIS
and
ROMA GILL

LONDON/A & C BLACK

NEW YORK/W W NORTON

Reprinted 1989
by A & C Black (Publishers) Limited
35 Bedford Row, London WC1R 4JH

ISBN 0-7136-3150-3

First published in this form 1976 by Ernest Benn Limited

© *Ernest Benn Limited 1976*

Published in the United States of America by
W. W. Norton and Company, Inc.
500 Fifth Avenue, New York, NY 10110

ISBN 0-393-90014-2 (USA)

A CIP catalogue record for this book
is available from the British Library

Printed in Great Britain

THE NEW MERMAIDS

The Atheist's Tragedy

THE NEW MERMAIDS

General Editor

BRIAN GIBBONS
Professor of English Literature, University of Zürich

CONTENTS

ACKNOWLEDGEMENTS

EVERY EDITOR of Tourneur's work must acknowledge the great debt to Allardyce Nicoll's edition of 1929, and more recently to the efforts of Irving Ribner for his edition in the Revels Series of plays (1964).

Sheffield   B. R. M.
November 1974   R. G.

INTRODUCTION

THE AUTHOR

MANY YEARS AGO Marcel Schwob began his 'Imaginary Life' of Cyril Tourneur with the extravagant claim that he was 'naquit d'un dieu inconnu avec une prostituée', but unhappily in our prosaic world such assertions are (unless accompanied by incontrovertible evidence) no longer acceptable.[1] The little we know about Tourneur must be pieced together from the handful of documents mentioning his name. Of his family we know, with certainty, nothing. A Captain Richard Turnor, who died about 1598, was in the service of the Vere and Cecil families, with whom the dramatist had a long association; this may indicate some connection, though hardly a very meaningful one. The date of his birth is unknown, and one can only guess at the decade 1570–1580. Much of his life seems to have been spent in the employ of the Veres and the Cecils, and it seems likely that a considerable portion of this was spent overseas, concerned with military and other affairs. In 1617 he was in some kind of trouble with the Privy Council, but was apparently rescued by the intervention of the Cecils. At the end of 1625 he joined Cecil's unhappy Cadiz expedition, was taken ill, and with many others put off the ship the *Royal Anne* at Kinsale in Ireland, where he died in February 1625/6. This much we know from a petition from 'Mary Turner wife of Cyrill Turner late deceased' who claimed that her husband, before the Cadiz exploit, 'was ymployed under the States of Holland, & had a settled meanes of 60^{li} p[er] annu[m] by his place, beside the dayly hopes he had of some greater p[re]ferment there'.[2]

Tourneur first appeared on the literary scene in 1600 with the publication of a long and obscure poem, *The Transformed Metamorphosis*, a satire of sorts showing the influence of Spenser and Marston but ultimately yielding up no very clear meaning. He is known to have written four other poems. 'A Griefe on the Death of Prince Henrie' was entered in the Stationers' Register in 1612 and printed with two other funeral elegies (by John Webster and Thomas Heywood) the following year. One of the Huntington Library copies also contains an eight-line poem 'On the Succession' which is signed

---

[1] *Vies imaginaires* (Paris, 1896), pp. 207–9. The passage is quoted in Nicoll (p. 1), which gives the fullest 'Life' and from which most of the present details are drawn.

[2] Nicoll, p. 31.

vii

'C.T.' but which was evidently suppressed in the course of printing. Two other poems, one a six-line epitaph, 'On the death of a child but one year old', and a longer one of eight seven-lined stanzas 'Of My Lady Anne Cecill, the Lord Burleigh's Daughter', testify more to Tourneur's duty to the Cecil family than to any poetic ability. Apart from these four, he is credited with 'A Funerall Poeme Upon the Death of the Most Worthie and True Souldier, Sir Francis Vere' (Stationers' Register, 1609) largely because of his known connection with the family. His association with the Cecils may have prompted a prose *Character of Robert Earle of Salesburye*, written and published soon after Robert Cecil's death in 1612. Another possibly genuine prose work is the blackletter pamphlet *Laugh and Lie Downe: or, the Worldes Folly*, which was printed in 1605 and bears the initials 'C.T.' appended to the dedication.

Following Vere's death in 1609 Tourneur seems to have tried his hand at some dramatic work for a few years. *The Atheist's Tragedy* was entered in the Stationers' Register in 1611 and published the same year. In the Register for February 1611–12 is an entry for 'A play booke beinge a Tragecomedye called, The Noble man, written by Cyrill Tourneur',[3] which was re-entered in September 1653 by Humphrey Moseley as 'The Nobleman, or Great Man, by Cyrill Tourneur'. The play was never published. Warburton claims to have had a manuscript of 'The Great Man T' or 'The Nobleman T.C' by 'Cyrill Turnuer' which was involved in what W. W. Greg called 'The Bakings of Betsy' – the papers destroyed by his cook when she used them under her pie bottoms.[4] Hazlitt wrote that 'Dr Furnivall told me many years ago that the MS. was in the hands of a gentleman at Oxford who was editing Tourneur's works: but I have heard nothing further of it'.[5] In 1613 Robert Daborne, one of Henslowe's hack dramatists, wrote to the impresario that he had 'given Cyrill Tourneur an act of ye Arreignment of london to write',[6] but this play, identified by Greg[7] with *The Bellman of London*, is now lost. Attempts to trace Tourneur's hand in *The Honest Man's Fortune*, first printed in the 1647 Folio of Beaumont and Fletcher, have not been successful; the stylistic evidence is very weak. The best, and most famous, play attributed to Tourneur is of course *The Revenger's Tragedy*, anonymously published in 1607. This date would anticipate Tourneur's brief and unspectacular foray into

[3] Arber, III, 478.
[4] 1911; reprinted in *Collected Papers of Sir Walter W. Greg*, ed. J. C. Maxwell (1966), p. 53.
[5] *A Manual for the Collector and Amateur of Old English Plays* (1892), p. 167.
[6] *Henslowe Papers*, ed. W. W. Greg (1907), p. 72.
[7] ibid., p. 75.

dramatic activity, but that in itself is not enough to discount his authorship. The play was first assigned to him by Edward Archer in 1656, and he was followed by Francis Kirkman in 1661. But serious doubts have been cast on the matter, and various other possible authors, chiefly Middleton, have been credited with this fine tragedy. The present editors, while not accepting the Middleton attribution, feel major qualms about admitting Tourneur's authorship.[8]

By the end of 1613 Tourneur had apparently given up hopes of a theatrical career and returned to government service. A record of 23 December 1613 mentions a payment of 40s for carrying letters to Brussels, and he subsequently received a pension from the United Provinces, the one whose loss his widow laments in her petition to 'the Lords, & others Com[m]ittees of his Ma[jestie]s hono[ra]ble Councell of Warr'.[9]

DATE

There is little point in manufacturing a date problem for *The Atheist's Tragedy* unless one believes that Tourneur wrote *The Revenger's Tragedy* and that the better work must have been the later. Fleay attempted to place it before the end of the siege of Ostend in 1604,[10] but Stoll was surely correct in pointing out that although this may date the action, it is no proof of the time of writing.[11] Reminiscences of *King Lear* – not least in the relationship between D'Amville and Shakespeare's Edmund – would suggest a date much closer to the original registration in 1611.

SOURCES

The very negation of action in *The Honest Man's Revenge* would be enough to deter scholars from searching for a plot for this play, and certainly no source for the main story of D'Amville, Charlemont, and Castabella has yet come to light. It may very well be that Tourneur read, in some collection of Italian or French *novelle*, a murder story which he utilized for the Montferrers episodes, and it

---

[8] For a comprehensive review of the authorship problem see the edition of *The Revenger's Tragedy* by R. A. Foakes (1966) which, while discussing the arguments with care and impartiality, acknowledges Nicoll's recommendation of the virtue of anonymity.

[9] Nicoll, p. 31.

[10] F. G. Fleay, *A Biographical Chronicle of the English Drama* (1891), II, 263.

[11] E. E. Stoll, *John Webster* (Boston, 1905), pp. 210–13.

is not impossible that personal experience of the siege of Ostend gave him the details for the more than usually heartfelt description of Charlemont's watch in II.vi. Two accounts of the siege would have been available to him. *A True Historie of the Memorable Siege of Ostend* was published in 1604, and Francis Vere's memoirs, although not printed as *The Commentaries of Sir Francis Vere* until 1657, would have been accessible in manuscript had the dramatist needed to make use of them. But the siege itself, except as a means of removing Charlemont temporarily from the scene, is of no major importance, and there are no signs of verbal borrowing from either of these sources.

The lusty comedy of Levidulcia's entanglement with Fresco and Sebastian in II.iii and v has analogues in plenty. Langbaine[12] suggested a novel from *The Decameron* (novel 6, day 7), but similar stories were widespread through the continent and England. *Tarletons Newes* (1590) recounts 'Why the Gentlewoman at Lyons sat with her hair clipt off in Purgatory'; Edward Sharpham used the same device in his *Cupid's Whirligig* (1607); it appears in *A World of Wonders* (1607) where the story is told by 'two Florentines'; and it forms most of the second act of *Women Pleased*, a Fletcher play of uncertain date.

THE PLAY

The Structuring of Themes

The Atheist's Tragedy is a study of Power: cosmic power, moral power, and the power of Reason to inform and direct human action. It does not offer deep insights into the psychology of heroic characters, it does not present the fates of men on whom the destinies of nations hang, it is not a vehicle for the passionate display of poetry and the assembled arts of language. It is, in some ways, a very plain play. It offers a thesis, and a demonstration of that thesis; it works out, with great singleness of purpose, the implications of a theoretical position which is stated in baldly conceptual language at the very beginning:

> Borachio, thou art read
> In Nature and her large philosophy.
> Observ'st thou not the very self same course
> Of revolution both in man and beast?   (I.i, 3–6)

Man, says D'Amville, is surely no more than a superior form of animal, differing in degree but not in kind from all other animals. Since 'this life comprehends our happiness' (I.i, 23), and there is

[12] *An Account of the English Dramatick Poets* (1691), p. 505.

no fear of a judgement hereafter, it follows that pleasure is man's only objective, and wealth the essential means to pleasure. Wealth has the additional advantage that it can be handed on to one's children, and in one's children lies the only immortality there is any need to consider. This is the creed D'Amville enunciates in conversation with Borachio for the first sixty lines of the play, and it would be difficult to cite another play in the whole range of Elizabethan and Jacobean drama with so undramatic and anti-theatrical an opening. The mode is conceptual, the method is uninterrupted dialogue, and the manner is that of philosophical exegesis. The only comparisons which offer themselves are the openings of Shakespeare's *Henry V*, Marlowe's *Doctor Faustus*, and Chapman's *Bussy D'Ambois*. Shakespeare's play begins with two scenes in which the council debate for over 300 lines the legitimacy of Henry's claim to lands in France. *Doctor Faustus* begins with a sixty-two line soliloquy in which Faustus reviews his past achieve-ments and assesses his intellectual position. At the opening of Chapman's play the hero enters and delivers a long soliloquy in which he rails against Fortune and bewails his state of poverty. Each play does set out the terms in which its story will develop, but Marlowe, Shakespeare, and Chapman, in different ways, make the enunciation of a theme a dramatic event. Marlowe, for example, telescopes the whole history of Faustus's education into a few telling images – Aristotle's *Analytics*, a volume of Galen, Jerome's Bible, and the like; he allows his hero a rich, cryptic poetic utterance, and he permits him direct address to the audience. The opening of Tourneur's play makes no such concessions to the art of the theatre. The two characters speak to each other, philosophically and realistic-ally. The emotions are not roused; only the intellect is engaged. Clearly, from the evidence provided in other parts of the play, this is a deliberate decision on the dramatist's part. The intention is to lay out, with the utmost clarity, and without the intrusion of narra-tive or emotion, the basic tenets of a philosophical position which is to be of the utmost importance in the development of the play.

It is important to notice that D'Amville does not begin by denying the existence of a supreme being. He is not an atheist in any crude and simple sense.[13] His creed is based on the observation that no 'god

[13] On atheistic ideology in this period see G. T. Buckley, *Atheism in the English Renaissance* (Chicago, 1932); E. A. Strathmann, 'Elizabethan Meanings of Atheism', in *Sir Walter Ralegh: A Study in Elizabethan Skepticism* (New York, 1951); P. H. Kocher, *Science and Religion in Eliza-bethan England* (San Marino, California, 1953); D. J. Palmer, 'Marlowe's Naturalism', in *Christopher Marlowe: New Mermaid Critical Commentaries* I, ed. Brian Morris (1968).

CYRIL TOURNEUR

hypothesis' is necessary to explain natural law. His method is scientific ('see', 'observe', 'read', 'show', 'consider' are key words in the opening lines), and the evidence is assembled in a detached, almost clinical, fashion. What Tourneur is presenting is a sketch of the typical philosophy of an Elizabethan Naturalist. Robert Ornstein has pointed out that 'it is not surprising that D'Amville should substitute a nature philosophy for religious faith; atheism and natural philosophy are consistently linked by many speculative writers in the period'.[14] Ornstein quotes Pierre de la Primaudaye's *The French Academie* as a typical example:

> Naturall philosophie consisteth chiefly in the Mathematicks, which are divided into many parts and particular sciences, of which the most of them seeme to manie not greatly necessarie, as that which intreateth of the nature of the heavens, of the sunne, of the moone, of their motions, measures, & of the naturall causes of al things. Which oftentimes serveth rather to content the curiositie of hawtie spirits, than to make them better, insomuch that sometimes, by speculations, and by vaine and frivolous questions, they seeke out the naturall causes of things so curiouslie, that in the end they strive to finde out another beginning of all things than GOD: whereby at length they remaine deceived and confounded in their knowledge, as both the writings of so manie ancient philosophers, and also the life of many in our time do proove unto us.[15]

Ornstein describes the Naturalist as 'a man of scientific outlook who viewed the universe as a purely material entity governed by physical laws of cause and effect, and who, being of an empirical turn of mind, would not accept the mysteries of religion even when confirmed by speculative reason'. This is very like the conclusion reached by E. A. Strathmann in his study of Elizabethan confutations of atheism, when he says that the atheist 'was likely to be a "naturalist" who, through overmuch study of nature, was inclined to exalt her, only the agent of creation, to the role of creator'. Obviously, D'Amville does not exhibit all the lineaments of the fully-fledged Naturalist, but this is surely the philosophical position he is created to represent, in however sketchy and incomplete a way. Tourneur creates the character, as any dramatist must, by implication and

---

[14] Robert Ornstein, '*The Atheist's Tragedy* and Renaissance Naturalism', *SP*, LI (1954), 194–207. See also L. I. Bredvold, 'The Naturalism of Donne in Relation to some Renaissance Traditions', *JEGP*, XXII (1923), 471–502, and R. Hoopes, *Right Reason in the English Renaissance* (Cambridge, Mass., 1962).

[15] Pierre de la Primaudaye, *The French Academie*, trans. T. B[owes] (1594), p. 39. On the importance of Primaudaye see F. A. Yates, *The French Academies of the Sixteenth Century* (1947).

suggestion rather than by setting out in full all the articles of the man's atheistic faith in due order. What is clear from the first scene is that D'Amville regards himself as the servant of Nature (the word accumulates meanings as the scene develops), that he allows no power above Nature, that he sees death as the end of all, and that wealth is therefore 'lord of all felicity'. The rest of the play is a narrative devoted to demonstrating the falsity and peril of this position. In order to gain wealth and pass it on to his posterity D'Amville commits murder, arranges for his nephew to be declared dead and disinherited, and arranges a marriage between his son Rousard and Castabella. But the murdered man reappears in ghostly form throughout the play,[16] the nephew returns, and, without violence, reclaims and regains his rights, the marriage of Rousard and Castabella is sterile, and D'Amville's plans all end in his own death and damnation. This sequence of events forms the backbone of the play, and it is the constant focus of the audience's attention. But it is not the only pattern which the play exhibits, and the relationship between this main story and the other events which the play relates is not so simple as the connection between a main plot and a sub-plot.[17]

The opening scenes offer what appears to be a strong and direct pattern of contrasts. The academic tone and hairsplitting of the dialogue between D'Amville and Borachio is interrupted by the entry of Charlemont whose one desire is to go off to the war and win honour.[18] He is thwarted by his father's disapproval and his own lack of means, and he plainly tells his uncle, D'Amville, so. D'Amville's attitude to his nephew is, from the first, ironic and subtly slighting. In his words of greeting he carefully 'places' the key concept of 'honour', which he reiterates throughout the scene:

> Noble Charlemont,
> Good morrow. Is not this the honoured day
> You purposed to set forward to the war? (I.i, 61–3)

Charlemont, at this stage, stands for honour and glory and the martial virtues, but he is never allowed to use such words in this scene. It is D'Amville who tells us that war is noble, that it is the 'first original

---

[16] It is worth noticing that, unlike the ghost in *Hamlet*, Montferrers's ghost is never thought to be the devil in disguise. See J. Dover Wilson, *What Happens in Hamlet* (Cambridge, 1935), pp. 51–86.

[17] The complex relationships between various plots in Elizabethan and Jacobean drama are discussed in William Empson's *Some Versions of Pastoral* (1935), chapter 2.

[18] The concept of Honour, an important idea with a constant presence in English Renaissance drama, is discussed in Curtis Brown Watson, *Shakespeare and the Renaissance Concept of Honor* (Princeton, 1960).

of all man's honour', and that Charlemont is 'the honour of our blood'. But the deflative irony of his words is made overt when he offers Charlemont money:

> Borachio, where's the gold?
> I'd disinherit my posterity
> To purchase honour. 'Tis an interest
> I prize above the principal of wealth. (I.i, 87–90)

Act I, scene ii opens with Charlemont's father trying to persuade his son not to go to war. It would be a dignified and tender exchange were it not for the fact that we know the whole departure has been engineered by D'Amville to further his own designs. The theme of honour and the pursuit of glory is not developed in opposition to the theme of D'Amville's atheism, since the atheist is shown to be the manipulator of the soldier. All the themes of the play are presented in this scene: Belforest arrives to say farewell to Charlemont, bringing with him Castabella (who remains when all have left to declare her love for Charlemont); Languebeau Snuffe (who consents to guard Castabella); and Levidulcia, who re-appears at the end of the scene and by her conversation makes it very clear that her dominant characteristic is unsatisfied and rampant lust. By developing all his major characters so early in the play Tourneur commits himself to a particular dramaturgy. The audience will not meet new people as the play goes on, but it will be concerned with the extended interaction of these initial groupings. Towards the end of the scene D'Amville, in conversation with Borachio, places his finger unerringly on the quality which distinguishes so many of the characters: they are not what they seem. He says of Languebeau Snuffe:

> . . . compare's profession with his life;
> They so directly contradict themselves
> As if the end of his instructions were
> But to divert the world from sin that he
> More easily might engross it to himself.
> By that I am confirmed an atheist. (I.ii, 208–13)

There is no logic in D'Amville's argument, one cannot deduce from human hypocrisy the non-existence of any transcendant power. Tourneur intends the reasoning to sound specious from a theological point of view, but it also serves to shed a new light on the other characters and groups. Charlemont and Castabella are chaste and honourable enough, but they are also pitifully innocent and trusting. The Puritan Languebeau Snuffe is revealed as a pious fraud, full of religious vocabulary and patently on the make.[19] Levidulcia cloaks

---

[19] He belongs with Ben Jonson's gallery of Puritans, especially Ananias and Tribulation in *The Alchemist*, and Busy in *Bartholomew Fair*.

faithlessness and promiscuity beneath conventional married respecta-
bility. D'Amville himself makes one in this dance, since he functions
as a secret plotter, and, like Iago, he is not what he seems to other
men. But to Borachio (and therefore to the audience) he has been
transparently open and plain, both in his statement of faith and in
his plotting. The pattern is that of the guller and the dupes, the
ringmaster putting the circus animals through their hoops. What
distinguishes D'Amville is his singleness of mind and purpose, his
clear thinking, and his lack of self-deception.

The play explores the power of this clear-sighted rationalism, and
especially its power to achieve certain limited, defined objectives –
notably wealth and grandchildren. D'Amville's philosophy and his
peculiar cast of mind are certainly equal to the demands of the mild
plotting necessary to murder Montferrers, exile Charlemont, and
secure the inheritance. D'Amville's rationalism can likewise take
care of what might be thought to be the expression of divine displeasure in the thunder and lightning after the murder (II.iv). It
is 'a mere effect of Nature', and he explains it scientifically. He can
even go so far towards superstition as to find metaphoric aptness
in it:

> 'Tis a brave noise, and methinks graces our
> Accomplished project as a peal of ordnance
> Does a triumph; it speaks encouragement. (II.iv, 152–4)

But even D'Amville's rationalism depends on a calculation of
probabilities, and this is sorely stretched by the accident and
coincidence of the scene in the graveyard (IV.iii). Confronted by a
death's head, he stares at it 'distractedly', and when he finds
Charlemont and Castabella sleeping peacefully with skulls as their
pillows, he is forced to admit:

> Sure there is some other
> Happiness within the freedom of the
> Conscience than my knowledge e'er attained to.
> (IV.iii, 285–7)

He finally disavows his atheistic creed not because he is presented
with any totally convincing argument but because the balance of
probabilities has at that time tilted that way. The final straw is the
death of Rousard. He says:

> Can Nature be
> So simple or malicious to destroy
> The reputation of her proper memory?
> She cannot. Sure there is some power above
> Her that controls her force.   (V.i, 100–4)

The argument is specious; it is perfectly possible that Nature is malicious,[20] and the truth or falsehood of that statement in no way forces a decision about the existence or non-existence of God. It is Tourneur's purpose to show that D'Amville's devotion to Reason does not always result in impeccable logic. Further, he does not allow D'Amville to reap the benefit of his discovery in the fifth act. At the trial of Charlemont and Castabella, D'Amville is consumed with curiosity about the source of their fortitude and calm. He begs the Judges that he should be given Charlemont's body after execution:

> I would find out by his anatomy
> What thing there is in Nature more exact
> Than in the constitution of myself.   (V.ii, 145–7)

Tourneur does not permit D'Amville, in this last scene, to make and take advantage of the obvious deduction. He does not repent, he dies by accident, and in the eyes of the audience he would therefore be doomed to eternal damnation. Tourneur does not raise the question of theological Despair, as Marlowe does in *Doctor Faustus*.[21] Faustus knows, and is repeatedly reminded, that if a sinner repents and turns to God, he will be saved, but he is so convinced that this general truth does not apply in his unique case that he can never bring himself to repentance. All the paraphernalia of the Good Angel and the Bad Angel, the mysterious Old Man, and the moments of agonized soliloquy are deployed about this point, and it forms a large part of the thematic material of Marlowe's play. Tourneur meticulously avoids this debate, and his play is, for that reason, far less 'religious' than Marlowe's. It is only after he has struck out his brains that the truth begins to dawn on D'Amville, and he dies before he can benefit by it. The pattern of the rationalist's progressive downfall is an important thematic strand in the play, and the rationalism is richly counterpointed by two minor patterns: the study of what happens to an ignorant and weakly man who is armed only with vague good-will, in the character of Rousard; and the moral fable of the fate which awaits the woman of unbridled lust, in the story of Levidulcia.

Thematic patterns do not always correspond directly with theatrical patterns. The ideas in *The Atheist's Tragedy* are presented

---

[20] A wide range of dualistic or Manichaean heresies was available to Tourneur. See J. P. Brockbank, *Marlowe: Dr. Faustus*, Studies in English Literature 6 (1962).

[21] See L. B. Campbell, '*Doctor Faustus*: A Case of Conscience', *PMLA*, LXVII (1952), 219–39. The case she discusses is dramatized in N. Woodes, *The Conflict of Conscience* (1581).

in a more or less uninterrupted linear progression, coming to a simple climax in the trial scene (V.ii). But the play on the stage has inner tensions, and points of lesser climax, which complicate the full unfolding of the dramatic action. The first of these occurs in Act II, scene i, and the whole of the first act leads towards it. The first scene of the play is, as we have observed, a static scene devoted to philosophical talk, first about Nature and then about Honour. The following scene presents all the remaining major characters, and very little actually happens. Act I, scene iii, makes a change of tone; Castabella is 'avoiding the importunity of Rousard', but once again the action is all verbal. It is not until Act I, scene iv that a decisive action takes place – the forced union of Castabella with Rousard. Act II opens with a 'spectacular' scene – a scene in which the resources of the stage are used to make a dramatic point by combining the spoken word with visual presentation. The stage direction requires 'Music. A banquet. In the night', and the forced and false celebration of Castabella's marriage with drums and trumpets and feasting is made the setting for Borachio's long discourse, falsely reporting the battle at Ostend and the death of the one person with whom Castabella would have liked to share a wedding feast, Charlemont. The scene, with its pattern of ironic contrasts, sums up the issues presented in the first act in a fully dramatic spectacle.

Similarly, the second act achieves a dramatic climax at the beginning of the third, with the funeral of Montferrers. The two processions, the dead march, the musket volleys, and the solemn epitaphs, create a powerful and significant statement on the stage, even though they do little to advance the plot or to develop the thematic material. In theatrical terms, of course, the most important scene in the play is the long scene in the graveyard (IV.iii). The spectacular effect of charnel house, graves, skulls, and the like on the stage is balanced by the almost burlesque effects of the various entrances and exits. People chase each other on and off stage, pop into the charnel house, and dress up as ghosts in false beards with all the gusto of a Feydeau farce. But burlesque is not in full control in this scene, because the focus of the audience's attention is on D'Amville, whose whole personal philosophy and code of behaviour is under severe challenge at this point by the coincidences and irrationalities with which he is faced. His attempt at incestuous rape on Castabella is not simply an act of foul lust. There is reason for it. Rousard has proved incapable of providing him with a grandson, and so, naturally, he sets about the task himself. He needs a grandson because he needs to hand on the wealth which it is his sole object to accumulate to his posterity. In D'Amville's view the end obviously justifies the means. But at the very moment when he is likely to get what he wants, he is confronted by Charlemont, who 'rises in the disguise and frights D'AMVILLE away' (IV.iii, 175). The effect on an audience is obvious: it is ludicrous and they will laugh at it. Yet some thirty lines later D'Amville enters 'distractedly' and his long speech about the death's head is wholly serious. As we shall see later, this pattern of contrasts is central to the construction of the play, but it is worth noticing that this 'mixed' scene, which is, in its extent and its visual impact, the theatrical climax of the play, comes well before the events of the plot achieve any denouement. There is a trough, three scenes long, before the trial scene of Act V, scene ii, and in that trough all the minor issues of the play are settled. Belforest forces the truth about Levidulcia out of Fresco; the Snuffe and Soquette episode is wound up; Sebastian, Belforest, Levidulcia, and Rousard all die; Montferrers' ghost appears for the last time. There is, indeed, more stage action in these three scenes than in the whole of the rest of the play, yet that action is still no more than incidental to the working-out of the main plot. Tourneur has deliberately and carefully arranged matters so that the spectacular scenes, the moments of theatrical climax, do not correspond to the climactic pattern of the thematic development. This gives great weight to the sense of accident, of randomness, or, perhaps, of Providence, at work in the affairs of men. Men strive to control events, but they seldom succeed for long. *The Atheist's Tragedy*, like God, moves in a mysterious way.

The Tradition of Revenge

There seems little danger that the historical importance of Kyd's *The Spanish Tragedy* will be underrated. It is customary, now, to refer to 'the Kydian tradition' in revenge plays written at the end of the sixteenth and the beginning of the seventeenth centuries, and the popular impression is that Kyd's play started a voluminous fashion. In fact, scarcely a dozen of the surviving plays really owe convincing allegiance to Kyd, and to talk, as Fredson Bowers does, of 'The School of Kyd' is to dignify as an institution what is really no more than a random association.[22] It is not easy to distinguish what later dramatists owed specifically to Kyd from the more pervasive influence of Seneca on the Elizabethan drama, though attempts have been made, by Thorndike and by Bowers (in a rather heavy-handed way), to establish the twelve characteristics of the 'basic Kydian formula'.[23] The revenge plays of the period cannot,

[22] The standard work on the Revenge tradition is still Fredson Bowers, *Elizabethan Revenge Tragedy* (Princeton, 1940).

[23] ibid., pp. 71–3.

perhaps, be analysed successfully in this rigorous, pseudo-scientific manner, since such analysis depends upon a premise of distinguishable influence; and it may well be that Kyd, Seneca, Elizabethan law, the Bible, the teaching of the Church, and wild imaginings about what went on in Italy are so inextricably bound together in these plays that there are limits as to what can be ascribed to the influence of what. However, any comparison of *The Spanish Tragedy* with *The Atheist's Tragedy* would suggest that one stands at the beginning of a tradition and the other near the end.

The idea of revenge in Kyd's play is all-pervasive and comparatively simple. As J. R. Mulryne has said:

> In an obvious way, the play's action is set in motion and sustained by revenge-intrigues: Andrea seeks revenge for his death in battle at the hands of Balthazar; Bel-imperia looks for vengeance for Andrea's, her lover's, death; Balthazar and Lorenzo seek revenge on Horatio for winning Bel-imperia's love; Hieronimo pursues vengeance for the murder, by Lorenzo and Balthazar, of his son Horatio. From these intrigues develops all the rest of the play's narrative.[24]

And he quotes Philip Edwards's remark: '*The Spanish Tragedy* is a play about the passion for retribution, and vengeance shapes the entire action'.[25] It is notable that, in Kyd's play, there is hardly any questioning of the morality of revenge. Elizabethan moralists, clerics, and lawyers had denounced it widely and regularly, and the denunciation had always been made in religious, social, or moral terms. This is no part of Kyd's concern. He uses the various revenges as simple dramatic means of organizing human conflicts, clashes, and aggressions. It is not ethical, but structural.

Precisely the opposite is true in *The Atheist's Tragedy*. Tourneur is concerned with the revenge ethic. The classic statement of the chief argument against revenge is made by Thomas Becon, in 1560:

> To desire to be revenged, when all vengeance pertaineth to God, as he saith, 'Vengeance is mine, and I will reward' . . . this to do ye are forbidden.[26]

Clearly, the words of holy writ precisely and specifically forbid the act of revenge: it is a sin. So it is surprising that neither *The Spanish Tragedy* nor any of the other tragedies of revenge in the sixteenth century depends upon a situation in which a hero is torn between his passion for a just vengeance and his Christian duty. It is not until

[24] J. R. Mulryne, ed., *The Spanish Tragedy* (The New Mermaids, 1970), p. xx.
[25] P. W. Edwards, ed., *The Spanish Tragedy* (Revels edition, 1959), p. li.
[26] Quoted by Bowers, op. cit., p. 13, from *The Early Works*, ed. Rev. John Ayre (Parker Society, 1843), p. 323.

The Atheist's Tragedy that any dramatist explores what might happen if a character took these Biblical words seriously, and tried to act in accordance with them. It is perhaps important to try to understand the context in which Tourneur and his contemporaries would have seen the phrase 'Vengeance is mine'. It occurs in the Song of Moses (Deuteronomy, 32, 35):

> Vengeance and recompence are mine; their foot shall slide in due time: for the day of their destruction is at hand, and the things that shall come upon them make haste.[27]

The Old Testament sense is that the sufferings of the children of Israel are but for a moment, and the arsenals of divine wrath will, in due time, be unleashed on their enemies. But the phrase is famous because it is quoted by St Paul in the Epistle to the Romans (12: 19):

> Dearly beloved, avenge not yourselves, but give place unto wrath: for it is written, Vengeance is mine: I will repay, saith the Lord.

The twelfth chapter of the Epistle catalogues the code of behaviour to which Christians should aspire, and St Paul exhorts them to think soberly, to be kindly affected one to another, to be not slothful in business, to recompense to no man evil for evil, and so on. In tone, style, and content it is very reminiscent of the Beatitudes in the Gospels.[28] The prohibition of revenge is not a simple, isolated command, it is subordinate to the real advice which immediately follows it: 'Therefore if thine enemy hunger, feed him; if he thirst, give him drink'. Tourneur's play resolutely avoids this area of ethical concern. There is no question that Charlemont is seeking by his patience and his forbearance to 'heap coals of fire' on the head of D'Amville, nor is there any suggestion, in action or imagery, that Castabella is the image of the Christian virgin and martyr who, by her suffering and example, wins her persecutors to the faith. Charlemont's actions are only nominally Christian: in many ways he owes far more to the Stoic tradition of patient endurance and fortitude. It would be a mistake to see *The Atheist's Tragedy* as in any obvious way a religious tract.

The revenge theme inevitably imposes certain structural problems on the dramatist who makes use of it. The most obvious difficulty is the interim between the moment in which the revenger becomes

[27] Although *The Atheist's Tragedy* and the Authorized Version of the Bible were published in the same year, 1611, Tourneur is most likely to have read his Bible in the Geneva version. Quotations are therefore from the Geneva version.

[28] See, for example, Matthew, 5: 3–12, 21–6, 38–48.

convinced of his duty and the moment he performs it. Shakespeare makes this gap cover the greater part of the action in *Hamlet*, and all other dramatists have to find reasons for this delay. Helen Gardner describes the most characteristic solution:

> ... in Elizabethan revenge plays it is not merely the initial situation which is created by the villain. The denouement also comes about through his initiative. It is not the result of a successfully carried out scheme of the revenger. The revenger takes an opportunity unconsciously provided for him by the villain. Given this opportunity, which he seems unable to create for himself, he forms his scheme on the spur of the moment. ... This conception of a hero who is committed to counter-action, and to response to events rather than to the creation of events, is very powerfully rendered by Tourneur in the exposition of *The Revenger's Tragedy*.[29]

In *The Atheist's Tragedy* Tourneur apotheosizes this technique of 'counter-action' by a device which frees the revenger from the necessity for action of any kind. Charlemont is not aware that he has anything to revenge until Act II, scene vi, when the Ghost of Montferrers appears to him, and says:

> Return to France, for thy old father's dead
> And thou by murder disinherited.
> Attend with patience the success of things,
> But leave revenge unto the King of kings. (II.vi, 19–22)

These are the play's key lines in establishing and directing the revenge theme. It has been suggested that the word 'patience' is used here 'in the religious sense of uncomplaining acceptance of fate as a manifestation of divine will, coupled with faith and hope in a future felicity promised by Christ',[30] but this is probably to particularize too far. Patience, although a recognized Christian virtue, has never been a matter of dogma, on a par with Faith, Hope, and Love; it has been regarded as a mode of life rather than a means of Grace.[31]

---

[29] Helen Gardner, *The Business of Criticism* (Oxford, 1959), pp. 41–3, and reprinted in *Shakespeare: Modern Essays in Criticism*, ed. L. F. Dean (Oxford, 1967, revised ed.). See also C. V. Boyer, *The Villain as Hero in Elizabethan Tragedy* (1914), 165–86.

[30] Ribner, p. 55.

[31] Although the play is sub-titled 'The Honest Man's Revenge', and we are told in the final scene that 'patience is the honest man's revenge', Tourneur offers very little exploration of the theme of Patience itself. The Bible distinguishes two forms of Patience: *makrothumia* (endurance, constancy, forbearance, long-suffering) and *hupomene* ('a remaining under', steadfastness, constancy, a patient waiting for). The difference is described by R. C. Trench, *Synonyms of the New Testament* (1854), III, 14: '*Makrothumia* will be found to express patience in respect of persons, *hupomene* in respect

The dramatic significance of the Ghost's words is to urge Charlemont to take no action, to suffer rather than to perform, and, in particular, not to initiate any kind of vengeance. The significance of *The Atheist's Tragedy* in the tradition of Elizabethan revenge plays lies in the fact that it is the first play in which a revenger is specifically forbidden to take revenge. There is a hint in *Hamlet*, when the Ghost instructs Hamlet to make an exception:

> . . . nor let thy soul contrive
> Against thy mother aught; leave her to heaven.

Claudius is another matter, and the command is imperious: 'If thou didst ever thy dear father love. . . . Revenge his foul and most unnatural murder'. It is surprising that no playwright before 1611 thought to make the Christian prohibition of revenge the theme of a play, especially since all the materials for complex inner conflict and prolonged narrative tension are obviously present in the situation. Such a play could have shown, at any length, the struggle within a man's mind as he strives to obey his conscience and control his natural passions. It is in some ways the weakest part of *The Atheist's Tragedy* that Tourneur fails to exploit fully the opportunities he has created for himself. Charlemont is not presented as a character torn by indecision and a prey to doubt. Indeed, his first appearance on his return to France is at his own funeral (III.i) where he finds Castabella mourning over his hearse, and addresses her with the imperishable line:

> Sweet Castabella, rise; I am not dead.   (III.i, 72)

---

of things. . . . We should speak, therefore, of the *makrothumia* of David (II Sam. 16: 10–13), the *hupomene* of Job (James 5: 11)'. *Hupomene* is the word used by St Paul in Romans 2: 7, when he contrasts 'patient continuance in well doing' with contentiousness, disobedience to the truth, obedience to unrighteousness, indignation, and wrath. A further stage of definition is offered later in the Epistle (15: 5) when St Paul writes: 'Now the God of patience and consolation grant you to be likeminded one toward another according to Christ Jesus'. One would expect Tourneur, who is quite precise and detailed about D'Amville's brand of atheism, to be equally detailed about Charlemont's patience. But this is not the case. Where he uses the word, Tourneur ascribes no precise (and certainly no theological) meaning to it (see, for example, III.i, 125; III.i, 145; III.iii, 28; III.iv, 43; V.ii, 153). The nearest he comes to describing the virtue is in Charlemont's speech at III.iii, 34 ff., where he speaks of suffering the blows of Fate with fortitude. There is a faint flavour of the Book of Job in his words, but, on the whole, the tone is Stoic. Not until the very end does Charlemont relate his patience specifically to the Grace of God, and the theme is not in any sense a dramatic counterweight to the naturalistic atheism of D'Amville.

Castabella swoons, and Charlemont berates himself for his lack of consideration. It is a small moment, but it does suggest that Charlemont is not to be thought of as a deep thinker, or a sensitive plant. He is a soldier, a man of honour, and a man of moral principle (in so far as there is any attempt to portray him with any degree of psychological truth). In Act III, scene ii, he is provoked to anger by Sebastian, and is about to kill him when the Ghost reappears and reminds him of his duty of patience. Charlemont's reply:

> You torture me between the passion of
> My blood and the religion of my soul   (III.ii, 35–6)

gives us some idea of the way in which the conflict might be played out, but Tourneur makes only this single gesture in that direction. Charlemont, in prison in the following scene, soliloquizes on his condition, but in the tone and manner of a man who is trying to work out a tricky problem rather than the accents of a sufferer on the rack:

> I grant thee, Heaven, thy goodness doth command
> Our punishments, but yet no further than
> The measure of our sins. How should they else
> Be just?   (III.iii, 1–4)

Charlemont is no theologian: ten minutes with the Book of Job would have taught him that his line of enquiry is not only fruitless, it is naïve. Tourneur, in his handling of the revenge theme, does not attempt to explore the inner recesses of any character's soul. He is far more concerned with outward display, with the demonstration – sometimes in quite sketchy terms – of a proposition and its necessary outworking. There is an almost Euclidian determinism about it. Given a character who is, by the conventions of society, entitled to exact revenge on a villain, what would happen if that character, in obedience to Biblical injunction, refused to exercise that right? There are two possible answers to the proposition. The first is exemplified in the crucifixion of Christ, when the chief priests derided him, saying 'He saved others; let him save himself, if he be Christ, the chosen of God'. Christ was not vindicated, he did not descend from the cross, and the mystery of unjustified suffering remains as one of the agonies of faith. The second, and simpler, answer is to show that 'he that shall endure to the end, the same shall be saved',[32] and to demonstrate that some unmerited suffering is strangely balanced by concomitant reward on this earth and in

[32] Matthew 24: 13. The whole twenty-fourth chapter, which is concerned with the theme of Christian endurance, makes Charlemont's case far more powerfully than Tourneur does.

this life. Tourneur holds resolutely to the second, optimistic, answer, and the play shows that the refusal to exact revenge can pay good dividends in the end. Charlemont ends the play united with Castabella, possessed of his inheritance, exonerated for any indiscretions he may have committed, and fully triumphant over his wicked uncle. Almost his last words in the play sum up his position:

> Only to Heaven I attribute the work,
> Whose gracious motives made me still forbear
> To be mine own revenger. Now I see
> That *patience is the honest man's revenge.*　　(V.ii, 275–8)

There is a sententiousness, almost a smugness, about these lines which is not helped by the words 'Now I see', which suggest that Charlemont is not only good, he is stupid. We may also detect a less than fully Christian altruism in the realization that by being a good boy Charlemont has achieved his full and bloody vengeance after all. And he does not seem in the least disturbed by his discovery.

In *The Spanish Tragedy* Kyd took up the Greek and Senecan ideas of revenge as the basis of his tragic structure. His revengers took their revenge, and it brought them to disaster. The pattern begun by an act of violence was completed by another.[33] But Kyd's plays, and those of his imitators, were performed and discussed in a country which owed at least nominal allegiance to the Christian faith, which not only specifically rejected the revenge ethic, but positively commanded men to love their enemies and to do good to them which despitefully use you and persecute you. The revenge theme was only available for a dramatist so long as no one wrote a play in which the Christian position was centrally adopted. Once Tourneur had written *The Atheist's Tragedy* there was nothing left for anyone to say on the subject. Revenge plays, of a kind, continued to be written after 1611, but they went over and over the old ground. There is a very real sense in which, with *The Atheist's Tragedy*, the Elizabethan revenge play, inaugurated so spectacularly by Kyd, committed a rational, predictable, and rather undistinguished suicide.

The Morality Tradition

At the end of the nineteenth century there was an appreciable rise in the critical interest given to Tourneur. It centred on *The Revenger's Tragedy*, but, by extension, *The Atheist's Tragedy* received its share of attention. The general sense, among critics like Symonds and Archer, was that the plays represented a rich decadence

---

[33] But see also Dorothea Krook, *Elements of Tragedy* (New Haven, 1969), especially pp. 1–34.

not unlike the 1890s themselves.[34] The frissons and the skulls of
Tourneur's plays found an echo in the sharp line and shocking
subjects of Aubrey Beardsley. It was not until 1938, when L. G.
Salingar published his essay on *The Revenger's Tragedy and the
Morality Tradition*[35] that the balance was corrected, and a judgement could be made of the two plays which was better informed and
more scholarly, and less *parti-pris*. Salingar pointed out the many
characteristics which linked Tourneur's plays with the Moralities
(the didactic intent, the symbolic disguisings, the 'sententious'
writing, and so on), but his first, and most powerful, point concerned
the presentation of character:

> The characters in the Moralities are personified abstractions and
> moral or social types, representing the main forces making for or
> against the salvation of the individual and social stability; they have
> no dramatic functions outside the doctrinal scheme. The actions
> on the stage are symbolic, not realistic, and the incidents are related
> to each other logically, as parts of an allegory, or as illustrations of
> the argument.

This is an important insight, and should warn any critic of Jacobean
drama who tries to analyse the characters of these plays in terms of
psychological consistency that he is guilty of trying to trap the wind
in a bag. But it should also remind us that *The Atheist's Tragedy* is
not precisely the same kind of play as *Everyman*. Tourneur uses
what he inherits from the Morality tradition, but he adapts it, and
uses it for purposes that are his own. The characters of *The Atheist's
Tragedy* are, to some extent, 'personified abstractions and moral or
social types', but they are not all abstractions, and abstractions is
not all they are. D'Amville is, of course, first and foremost the
exemplar of a philosophical position. He is a Naturalist, a rationalist,
and therefore an atheist. The whole tradition of English drama
required that such a man should therefore be a villain. The initial
contract which a dramatist establishes with his audience in the
opening minutes of the play makes this clear. Act I, scene i shows
D'Amville as precisely this kind of villain. And it tells us almost
nothing else. We do not learn, in that scene or elsewhere, anything
about D'Amville's background, his motivation, or his personality.
For example, we know he has two sons, Sebastian and Rousard, but
we never learn anything about their mother. Neither does Tourneur

---

[34] See, for example, the Introduction to *Webster and Tourneur*, ed. J. A.
Symonds, Mermaid series (1893).
[35] This important and highly influential study appeared first in *Scrutiny*,
VI (March 1938), 402–24. It is reprinted in *Elizabethan Drama: Modern
Essays in Criticism*, ed. R. J. Kaufmann (New York and Oxford, 1961).

allow D'Amville any kind of development as a character throughout the play. With the exception of his volte-face in the last scene he ends the play exactly as he began it. He does not suffer and he does not learn. We have already noticed that much the same could be said about Charlemont. He represents that blend of Stoic endurance and Christian patience which is necessary to exemplify 'the honest man's revenge', and Tourneur does not burden him with other, unnecessary personal qualities. There is a rudimentary sense that he is not particularly well-endowed with intelligence and native wit, that he is a good soldier, a loyal fellow, and a faithful lover, but that is all. His love scene with Castabella (III.i) is a rather impersonal rehearsal of the commonplaces, and Castabella herself is presented, from the beginning of the play to the end, as the picture of faithfulness, chastity, and self-wounding love. Tourneur enforces this stylization, this depersonalization in his presentation of character, by the stylization of each character's language. Castabella, for instance, in her soliloquy which begins Act II, scene iii, speaks in a philosophical, vocative, rarified, and representative way, which makes no attempt to mime the movement of a puzzled and suffering woman's mind:

> O love, thou chaste affection of the soul,
> Without th' adult'rate mixture of the blood,
> That virtue which to goodness addeth good,
> The minion of Heaven's heart. Heaven, is't my fate
> For loving that thou lov'st, to get thy hate?
> Or was my Charlemont thy chosen love. . . .
>
> (II.iii, 1–6)

Clearly, Tourneur is concerned here to stylize emotion. He is working within a mixed convention, which permits him to move quite long distances between the impersonal and the natural styles, but at this point we encounter him at his most rigidly stylized.[36] Here, his art is closest to the Morality tradition. It is less clear how we are intended to place a character like Levidulcia. It would be easy to say that she represents the medieval character of Lust, and nothing more. But within the context of this play she is clearly intended to be a deliberate opposite to Castabella. In Act II, scene iii, Castabella's soliloquy is immediately followed by the entry of Levidulcia, Rousard, Cataplasma, Soquette, and Fresco, and Levidulcia's first words change the tone completely:

[36] From this point of view (and from others) it is useful to compare Tourneur's dramatic technique with Webster's. See Inga-Stina Ekeblad, 'The "Impure Art" of John Webster', *RES*, IX (1958), 253–67. This essay is reprinted in the collection edited by Kaufmann, mentioned above, and elsewhere.

Mistress Cataplasma, good night. I pray when your man has brought you home, let him return and light me to my house. (II.iii, 15–17)

Throughout the play Levidulcia's sexual appetite is contrasted with Castabella's chaste and spare diet, but our response is not a simple opposition of approval and disgust. Act II, scene v follows the scene in which Montferrers is murdered by Borachio and D'Amville, and in it Levidulcia is about to be 'manned' by Fresco when they are interrupted by Sebastian. Fresco is pushed into the closet, and Sebastian is about to begin his welcome assault when Levidulcia's husband, Belforest, knocks at the door. The whole scene, which might have come from an Italian *novella*, and which is based on a story with a wide circulation in European folklore, is in an entirely different moral key from the scenes which surround it. We are invited to admire Levidulcia's wit and resourcefulness, and we are not asked to judge her morals, or Sebastian's. G. Wilson Knight comments aptly on this presence in the play:

> There is also a deflating of lust nausea, both in the worldly-wise acceptance of sexual instincts by Levidulcia and in that forecast of Sheridan's Charles Surface, the attractive, warm-hearted, generous yet licentious, young Sebastian.[37]

It is only Sebastian and his brother Rousard who show any change or development of character in this play. Sebastian begins the play as a careless young lecher, but he is appalled by the forced marriage of Castabella to Rousard, and, while never failing to pursue his own sexual advantage, he labours to defeat his father's plots by releasing Charlemont from prison. He dies in Act IV, scene v attempting to save the honour of Levidulcia against the rage of her husband. In his last moments he almost achieves heroism, of a quaint kind. Similarly, Rousard, at the beginning of the play, looks like the conventional figure of the weakling young man whose lecherous desires are vastly in excess of his possibility of performance. His pursuit of Castabella in Act I, scene iii, is pathetic. But after the so-called marriage he begins to exercise a resigned tenderness and an understanding towards his wife which goes far beyond the requirements of the role he represented in Act I. At the end of Act III, scene iv, there is an exchange between them which, in its delicacy and dignity, owes nothing to the Morality tradition and everything to Tourneur's sensitive observation of the way human beings can, in some circumstances, respond to one another:

---

[37] G. Wilson Knight, *The Golden Labyrinth* (1962), pp. 102–3. Knight's brief account of *The Atheist's Tragedy* is original, unusual, and stimulating.

ROUSARD
    . . . Credit me, my love,
I pity thy ill fortune to be matched
With such a weak unpleasing bedfellow.
CASTABELLA
    Believe me, sir, it never troubles me.
I am as much respectless to enjoy
Such pleasure as ignorant what it is.   (III.iv, 67–72)

Moments like these suggest the tone of Ford's tragedies rather than the mood of the Morality plays. But, on the whole, it is probably true to say that the characters of *The Atheist's Tragedy* are not presented as integrated, psychological entities, responding to their circumstances, and developing to accommodate them. D'Amville, Charlemont, and Castabella, in particular, are closer to being 'personified abstractions' than to being studies in the uniqueness of personality, and this has its effect on the development of the play's story. There is, however, one link between the play and the Morality tradition which cannot be ignored. It concerns the presentation of the character of D'Amville and the way in which we are encouraged to respond to him. All the Elizabethan writers on Atheism stress the horror of that creed: the atheist is a monster, a villain, a damned soul, an enemy of all that is lovely, or beautiful, or of good report. Yet D'Amville is no such creature. His clarity of mind, his singleness of purpose, and his avoidance of unnecessary hypocrisy compel our admiration. And, above all, despite his wickedness, he is capable of grim wit and unholy humour. He stands by the gravel pit in which Montferrers has been murdered, and handles the stone which has smashed his skull, and announces:

Upon this ground I'll build my manor house,
And this shall be the chiefest corner-stone. (II.iv, 99–100)

At moments like this, and there are many of them in the play, D'Amville clearly has allegiances with the Vice figure of the Moralities. F. P. Wilson has described the figure and function of the Vice:

Whatever else the Vice may be, he is always the chief comic character. . . . But in a substantial group of plays written and performed during the third quarter of the [sixteenth] century, the Vice, while always comic, is not merely comic. He possesses many of the characteristics of the comic vices in the earlier morality plays. He is not the devil but he is the devil's disciple, he is responsible to the devil for the seduction of men and women, he is the leader of minor vices, and he meets with a bad end.[38]

[38] F. P. Wilson, *The English Drama 1485–1585*, ed. G. K. Hunter (Oxford, 1969), pp. 59–62.

The lineaments of D'Amville are recognizable in this portrait, though it is significant that while D'Amville could be said to be the devil's disciple, the devil himself has no part or presence in the play. The supernatural world is represented only by one Ghost and assorted claps of thunder. D'Amville fulfils all the functions of the Vice, including the comic role, but his master remains resolutely off the stage.

Where there is so little development of character, and where so much depends upon formal exposition and contrast, one might expect the play to sag in the middle. It is an accusation that has been levelled against greater plays than *The Atheist's Tragedy* that the Morality tradition causes this failure at the centre. But the central scenes of Tourneur's play are tightly controlled and full of interest, and it is not difficult to find the reason. The opening scenes developed (as in chess) all the major characters, and so the dramatist, having posited D'Amville's atheism and his plots, is free to exploit the positions of his other characters and to build up significances and relationships. Thus, D'Amville's honesty is counterbalanced by the hypocrisy of Languebeau Snuffe; Castabella's purity is opposed by Levidulcia and her friends. And the central scenes of the play are concerned with the interactions of the several sub-plots. Levidulcia, Sebastian, Fresco, Cataplasma, Soquette, and Snuffe pursue their respective ways until a great number of them come together with the major characters in the large-scale and spectacular 'graveyard' scene (IV.iii). This multiple plotting maintains action and interest in the middle of the play, and contributes subtly towards the play's movement to its thematic climax. It is important to register the presence in *The Atheist's Tragedy* of other, older, dramatic traditions, since its 'mixed' dramaturgy might otherwise permit irrelevant critical questions to be raised. One might, for example, on purely naturalistic grounds, condemn Charlemont as a brutal legalistic opportunist when he interrupts D'Amville's dying confession in Act V, scene ii, with the brisk phrase:

> I claim the just advantage of his words.

But in the context of the whole scene, and of the tradition from which it comes, we are witnessing the personified abstraction of Good Deeds in his moment of final triumph over the devil's disciple. Nineteenth-century naturalism would see Charlemont as a tactless boor; in the light of the medieval Morality tradition we see the moment as part of the proper satisfaction that the Psalmist records when the wicked fall into the pit they have digged for others. The righteous shall rejoice at it.

Just as it would be erroneous to see *The Atheist's Tragedy* as unrelated to the past, and to the tradition of revenge plays and Moralities, so it would be a mistake to think of it as simply a stock exercise on commonplace themes. Muriel Bradbrook points out that Tourneur is not a slavish imitator:

> Tourneur's plays are easy of interpretation on the surface, because they are written in the Revenge convention, though he modified it in a manner peculiarly his own. His plays are closest to Marston's, not only in time but in temper.[39]

And at the end of her account of Tourneur's work she compares *The Atheist's Tragedy* with *The Revenger's Tragedy* (assuming Tourneur's authorship of both):

> It is true that there is a perceptible slackening of tension in *The Atheist's Tragedy*. The writing is on the whole less forcible, the vocabulary less pungent and concentrated. It is a *drame à thèse*, but less complex and more purely intellectual in its central theme.[40]

The phrase 'drame à thèse' is shrewd. There is something about the rigorous logic and the stylization of emotion in *The Atheist's Tragedy* which looks forward to the French theatre of the seventeenth century more than it looks back to anything at all.

The Mixture of Styles

The mixture of traditions in *The Atheist's Tragedy* is matched by a strange blend of styles. There are moments when we feel the force of traditional tragedy, and there are moments which are close to farce. The graveyard scene is almost burlesque and the trial scene is not far from melodrama. This mixture of comedy and tragedy, complicated by various forms of irony, and some moments of stage presentation which seem to derive from a symbolic and iconographic tradition, create a major problem of tone. In problems of this kind literary criticism cries out for aid to the theatre: any producer must attempt a solution to the overall question of tonal dominance, and must convince an audience that his solution is acceptable. Unfortunately, there has been no public, professional production of *The Atheist's Tragedy* in Britain in this century, and so we are denied the evidence that only the theatre can provide.

The problem can be epitomized in Act III, scene i. D'Amville enters with the funeral of Montferrers. We know that D'Amville is responsible for the murder, but this is a public scene and we allow that we shall be witnessing simulated grief. He speaks for six lines,

---

[39] M. C. Bradbrook, *Themes and Conventions of Elizabethan Tragedy* (Cambridge, 1935), p. 165.
[40] ibid., p. 184.

and then a stage direction orders 'A dead march. Enter the funeral of Charlemont as a soldier'. Again, there is the stage spectacle of the solemn rituals of death, but we are even more conscious that things are not what they seem, because we know that Charlemont is alive. D'Amville reads the epitaph of Montferrers, and then the epitaph of Charlemont, and then speaks in his own person for eighteen lines, beginning as follows:

> O might that fire revive the ashes of
> This phoenix! Yet the wonder would not be
> So great as he was good and wondered at
> For that. His life's example was so true
> A practique of religion's theory
> That her divinity seemed rather the
> Description than th' instruction of his life.
> And of his goodness was his virtuous son
> A worthy imitator.   (III.i, 35–43)

The tone is full, noble, and serious. If one read the lines out of context, they would betray no hint of irony. Yet the words D'Amville utters are totally contradicted by everything he stands for. The irony is a stage irony: a total contrast between the speaker and his words. But the tone is complicated even further by D'Amville's acknowledgement of the position. As he finishes his eulogy, the gunners or musketeers fire the third volley, and D'Amville says:

> 'Tis done. Thus fair accompliments make foul
> Deeds gracious. . . .   ·   (III.i, 49–50)

It cannot be that D'Amville believes this last statement; he is too clear-minded and too far from self-deception for that. But his hypocrisy would be clear to any audience from a much shorter scene. In the scene as we have it, Tourneur gives full and solemn value to the theatrical spectacle of the funeral, and the words uttered on the stage are in full tonal accord with the ritual they accompany. The irony is pervasive and dominant, but it is essentially implicit. The devil's disciple is marvellously in sympathy with the sons of light.

The same implicit irony is seen elsewhere in the play, and especially in the trial scene (V.ii). There, the overt ritual is that of the terrestrial tribunal trying a criminal case.[41] The only question at issue is whether or not Charlemont is guilty as charged. But as the scene develops, we become aware of another trial being conducted simultaneously. D'Amville is himself being arraigned before an invisible heavenly court to answer for his philosophy and his lifestyle. The most powerful witnesses against him are Charlemont and

---

[41] cf. the final scene of Jonson's *Volpone*.

Castabella, who, by their faith and their fortitude, show his philosophy to be erroneous and damnable. D'Amville is consumed by curiosity to know their secret, and he begins to take over the conduct of the proceedings. He begs his nephew's life, and wants to make him his physician. He talks to Charlemont about fortitude in the face of death, until the Second Judge says:

> Your lordship interrupts the course of law. (V.ii, 176)

The irony is complete. When the trial scene begins, D'Amville is not required to say a word, but so unbelievable is the spectacle before him that he must put it to the question, and by so doing he betrays himself and damns himself. Charlemont, like Shakespeare's Antony, is willing to risk all for love; D'Amville risks and loses all for curiosity.

The manner of his death, striking out his own brains with the executioner's axe, is ironic, but it is more than that. There is a symbolic, emblematic quality about the stage-picture of the villain hoist with his own petard, the self-executed executioner, the moral charade. It is the kind of thing one might expect to find in one of the Renaissance Emblem books,[42] accompanied by some motto about purposes mistook falling on the inventor's head. And there are several previous moments in the play when Tourneur makes specific use of this emblematic, pictorial technique. The first, and the most extensive, is at the opening of Act IV, when Cataplasma and Soquette moralize upon their needlework:

> ... What's here? A medlar with a plum tree growing hard by it, the leaves o' the plum tree falling off, the gum issuing out o' the perished joints, and the branches some of 'em dead and some rotten, and yet but a young plum tree. (IV.i, 2–5)

This picture is applied and moralized, and the ladies are joined by Sebastian, who discusses with them the morality of their emblems for more than fifty lines. The scene is full of light sexual innuendo, and many of the comparisons have oblique reference to the themes and situations of the play, but the dramatic effect is to halt the action for a moment and place before the audience a series of visual examples of the orthodox morality in which the action is set. A similar purpose is served by the skulls, the charnel house, and the ghostly impedimenta in Act IV, scene iii. D'Amville is moved to a meditative soliloquy of some thirty lines when he picks up one of the skulls. In the play's final scene Charlemont calls for a glass of water, and D'Amville for a glass of wine, which, as soon as he receives it, seems to turn to blood in his hands. In each case, the dramatic point

---

[42] See Russell A. Fraser, *Shakespeare's Poetics in relation to King Lear* (1962).

is made by the impact of the spectacle on the audience, and it is reinforced by the words which are spoken. This emblematic technique is found in *The Revenger's Tragedy*, and it is not uncommon in the plays of Webster, and Chapman, and Ford. In *The Atheist's Tragedy* its effect is to introduce moments of moral earnestness and reflection into the action, and sometimes these moments contrast strongly with the surrounding ironies.

T. S. Eliot, in one of his less felicitous phrases, described Tourneur as 'a highly sensitive adolescent with a gift for words'.[43] So far as *The Atheist's Tragedy* is concerned, Tourneur's language is not the most striking effect the play has on an audience or a reader. There are occasional flashes, as, for example, when Borachio describes how he murdered Montferrers (II.iv):

> . . . ere his faltering tongue
> Could utter double O, I knocked out 's brains
> With this fair ruby . . .   (II.iv, 92–4)

He is referring to the rock, covered in blood, which he holds in his hands. But apart from a few baroque, Websterian moments like this, the general quality of Tourneur's language is grave, weighty, and uniform. We may take a short speech by D'Amville, which occurs only a few lines later:

> Ay, mark the plot. Not any circumstance
> That stood within the reach of the design
> Of persons, dispositions, matter, time,
> Or place, but by this brain of mine was made
> An instrumental help, yet nothing from
> Th' induction to th' accomplishment seemed forced
> Or done o' purpose, but by accident.   (II.iv, 103–9)

The language is conceptual, but plain, the verse is loose and ranging, the syntax is periphrastic yet exhaustive. The passage is full of nouns. Tourneur's habitual style (which is best examined in an unimportant, descriptive passage like this one) is not given to adjectival excess, nor does he strain after verbal paradox or aphorism. Indeed, he largely avoids the arts of language, and he uses words with something far closer to a philosopher's regard for precision. This is not to say that Tourneur's imagination does not work in images. The imagery of the play has been extensively analysed by editors and critics. Una Ellis-Fermor, for instance, distinguishes four main categories: the 'building' imagery, the imagery based on 'kingship and the apparatus of government', upon 'business and financial transactions', and upon

---

[43] 'Cyril Tourneur', in *Selected Essays* (3rd edition, 1951), p. 189.

'outdoor nature in the specialized form of water and river imagery'.[44] These images are certainly present, but they are not obtrusive; the reader is not conscious, as he is when reading Webster, of a rich profusion which almost causes the imagination to surfeit. Inga-Stina Ekeblad has noticed that Tourneur's images do not strike us with an emotional force, but rather give 'clarifying amplification' to the meaning of a passage.[45] The truth of this phrase may be demonstrated from one of the most intense moments of the play, D'Amville's soliloquy in Act IV, scene iii:

> Why dost thou stare upon me? Thou art not
> The skull of him I murdered. What hast thou
> To do to vex my conscience? Sure thou wert
> The head of a most dogged usurer,
> Th' art so uncharitable. And that bawd,
> The sky there, she could shut the windows and
> The doors of this great chamber of the world,
> And draw the curtains of the clouds between
> Those lights and me about this bed of earth,
> When that same strumpet, Murder, and myself
> Committed sin together.   (IV.iii, 212–22)

The first three lines are bare of reference, and line four produces the plain figure of the 'dogged usurer'. The skull (because it does nothing but stare) is as uncharitable as a moneylender: a moneylender is 'dog-like' in that he is servile, untrustworthy, and despised, but the word 'dogged' also means 'persistent'. Persistence is a quality common amongst moneylenders, and one which unites them with this skull, since it stares persistently. The image amplifies and clarifies the initial picture of the skull, but it does not involve and extend the imagination. In the same way, the next seven lines offer a straightforward comparison, and nothing more. The sky is a bawd, the world is a chamber, the clouds are the curtains, the earth is a bed, and Murder is the strumpet. It is neat, and clear, but we are more impressed by its ingenuity than its imaginative power or its verbal complexity. When Hamlet holds a skull in his hand, his mind flashes from Yorick to painted ladies, to Alexander the Great, to bungholes, to Caesar, to a patch in a wall. Tourneur's imagination is more logical, more controlled. He uses images to explain and enforce what he means.

There is one character, however, who stands out from the others in respect of his language: Languebeau Snuffe. It may well be that

---

[44] Una Ellis-Fermor, 'The Imagery of *The Revengers Tragedie* and *The Atheists Tragedie*', *MLR*, XXX (1935), 289–301.
[45] Inga-Stina Ekeblad, 'An Approach to Tourneur's Imagery', *MLR*, LIV (1959), 489–98.

Tourneur here felt he had the backing of popular sanction. Snuffe speaks the seventeenth-century Puritan jargon, just as every stage-Puritan did. Tourneur is here very much like Ben Jonson, whose Puritan characters in *The Alchemist* and *Bartholomew Fair* produced such powerful mockeries of the typical speech of the saints. It was when a Puritan was concerned, in speech or print, to declare his (and God's) wrath against something that he typically produced the sort of language the dramatists found it easy to mimic. Daniel Wight, of Stretton, for example, a powerful and painful preacher of God's word, had this to say about bishops:

> Let my tongue cleave to the roof of my mouth, let all God's graces forsake me if I cease to pray and preach against the corruption of bishops – I mean the [e]state itself, and all their confederates, especially their new creatures, that is our vile servile dunghill ministers of damnation, that viperous generation, those scorpions. We build up the battered and scattered walls of Jerusalem, howsoever for a while Babel build itself, which I trust shortly shall prove Babel, even miserable confusion.[46]

In imitating this vituperative richness, Tourneur's Snuffe makes use of the vocabulary, but little else:

> Fie, fie, fie, these carnal kisses do stir up the concupiscences of the flesh.
> (I.ii, 121–2)

And from his first entrance his principal speech characteristic is a fairly simple exaggeration:

> I salute you both with the spirit of copulation. I am already informed of your matrimonial purposes, and will be a testimony to the integrity of your promises.
> (I.ii, 103–5)

There is nothing anywhere in Snuffe's language which has anything like the explosive poetic power of Jonson's Ananias, when he offers a rebuke:

> Lewd, superstitious, and idolatrous breeches....
> ... Thou look'st like Antichrist in that lewd hat.

But the greater restraint in the verbal characterization of Snuffe is of a piece with the comparatively subdued quality of Tourneur's writing elsewhere in the play. *The Atheist's Tragedy* is not a rhetorical diploma piece. Tourneur uses language always to mediate meaning, never to decorate it. The coolness, the intellectualism, the sense of detachment which one senses in the conduct of the plot, informs the language as well. The play is all of a piece throughout.

[46] Quoted and discussed in Patrick Collinson, *The Elizabethan Puritan Movement* (1967), p. 389.

This sense of the ultimate integrity of the play exists despite the many external influences which have been detected. It is very probable that one of the reasons which moved Tourneur to write *The Atheist's Tragedy* was the need to reply to Chapman's *Bussy* plays.[47] It is also quite possible that Tourneur had Marlowe's *Doctor Faustus* in mind at several points in the play: both are, amongst other things, studies in damnation.[48] But many other influences can be detected. Sebastian's soliloquy at the end of I.iv is remarkably like a similar situation in Marston's *The Malcontent*, the temptation of Castabella in III.iv is obviously based on the temptation of Isabella in *Measure for Measure*, and the opening of Act V owes everything to the first scene of Jonson's *Volpone*. But the greatest single influence is Shakespeare. It has been argued that the whole main plot of *The Atheist's Tragedy* is a deliberate attempt to provide a Christian answer to the problem of revenge as it is stated in *Hamlet*,[49] and there are many points of contact between the two plays. There are reminiscences of *Macbeth* in Tourneur's presentation of D'Amville, and correspondences have been traced between *The Atheist's Tragedy* and *King Lear*.[50] In some ways, the play reads like a patch-work, a tissue of allusions and references, a hotch-potch of other men's work. But this impression is superficial; it concerns only the details of presentation. If Tourneur is compared with Massinger (who rifled other dramatists for situations, images, phrases, and characters with a fine abandon), it will be seen that Tourneur does not borrow from other authors, he meditates on situations he knows from other dramatic contexts, and then re-enacts them. As evidence of this technique one might cite the fact that there are remarkably few direct verbal borrowings in *The Atheist's Tragedy*. One is often reminded of other plays, but by similarities in situation, not by identical words.

The Atheist's Tragedy is tragic only in a loose sense. At the end there is no sense of the sadness of great waste, nor is there regret at the inevitability of it all. We have not watched a noble man fall from happiness to disaster, nor have we traced the working-out of 'some vicious mole of nature' in an otherwise heroic protagonist. We have not seen a great act of shame visited with disproportionate suffering which issues in an ultimate wisdom. The play is not

---

[47] See Clifford Leech, '*The Atheist's Tragedy* as a Dramatic Comment on Chapman's *Bussy* plays', *JEGP*, LII (1953), 525–30.
[48] See Ribner, p. lxiii.
[49] See D. J. McGinn, *Shakespeare's Influence on the Drama of his Age* (New Brunswick, N.J., 1938), 30–7. See also Ribner, p. lxiv.
[50] See Robert Ornstein, *The Moral Vision of Jacobean Tragedy* (Madison, Wisconsin, 1960), p. 121.

conceived on this scale. In form, it is a 'thesis-play' more commonly found in French drama than in English. It presents the audience with a monstrous proposition (the denial of God's providence) in quite matter-of-fact terms, and works out the consequences of misbelief with clear and ruthless logic. In content, it is a study of power, and the limits of power. The blunt truth which the play proclaims is that no man can defy the power of God, and live. Yet D'Amville is neither Faustus nor Icarus, and we can view his fall (and Charlemont's vindication) with a strangely academic detachment. The abiding impression which *The Atheist's Tragedy* leaves is of a bold and important experiment – which didn't quite come off.

ABBREVIATIONS

Arber   *A Transcript of the Registers of the Company of Stationers of London*, ed. Edward Arber (1875–94).

Collins   *The Plays and Poems of Cyril Tourneur*, ed. John Churton Collins (1878).

JEGP   *Journal of English and Germanic Philology*.

MLR   *Modern Language Review*.

Nicoll   *The Works of Cyril Tourneur*, ed. Allardyce Nicoll (1929).

OED   *The Oxford English Dictionary*.

PMLA   *Publications of the Modern Language Association of America*.

Q   The first Quarto (1611–12).

RES   *Review of English Studies*.

Ribner   *The Atheist's Tragedy*, ed. Irving Ribner, The Revels Plays (1964).

s.d.   stage direction.

SP   *Studies in Philology*.

Tilley   M. P. Tilley, *A Dictionary of the Proverbs in England in the Sixteenth and Seventeenth Centuries* (Ann Arbor, 1950).

NOTE ON THE TEXT

THERE ARE IN EXISTENCE twenty-one copies of the first Quarto of *The Atheist's Tragedy*, some bearing the date 1611 and others, although clearly from the same printing, 1612. All collate A¹, B–K⁴, L³. The text is, on the whole, carefully printed, with the five acts precisely marked (but with no scene division) and with exits and entrances clearly indicated. Some of the stage directions appear to be authorial, such as that introducing Act I, scene iii: *Enter* CASTABELLA, *avoiding the importunity of* ROUSARD. Others, however, bear the marks of a theatrical hand – the curt *The Scarfe* at II.i, 105, for instance.

The one major problem facing the editors of this play is to discriminate between passages of prose and verse. Sometimes the solution is simple: no one would deny that Charlemont's meditation on Death the Leveller (IV.iii, 3–24) must be intended as verse, although Q prints it as prose. The dignity of the court scene (V.ii) seems to allow both Cataplasma and Fresco to speak out of their usual prose, while the Sergeant and the Musketeer in II.vi move from prose to verse depending upon whom they are addressing. But two characters remain obstinately 'prosaic' – Sebastian and Snuffe. Sebastian makes a fine contrast with Charlemont in the prison redemption scene (III.iii); and incidentally makes it imperative that Charlemont's speech at the end of this scene is restored as verse. Snuffe is a somewhat different matter. The copies of Q1 show three stages of printing: the uncorrected, the partially corrected, and what we must accept as the finally corrected. In one copy (Newberry) the lines printed in this edition as I.ii, 103–5 appear as verse:

> I salute you both with the spirit of copulation,
> I am already informed of your matrimoniall
> Purposes, and will be a testimonie to the integritie.

In other copies this has been corrected to prose – as in BM.C.34.e.10:

> I salute you both with the spirit of copulation, I am already informed of your matrimoniall purposes, and will be a testimonie to the integritie.

It has been suggested by Dr Giles E. Dawson of the Folger Library that a fault in the type made it impossible for the words here to take the ink properly, and that the proof-reader must have seen that the passage was still incorrect, since the words 'I am' and 'be a' are badly blurred. So a third stage of revision seems to have occurred, producing the passage as it now reads in almost every copy:

> I salute you both with the spirit of copulation, I am already informed of your matrimoniall purposes, and will be a testimonie to the integritie of your promises.

The importance of this is, we think, that Snuffe must *always* appear as a 'prose' character (except of course on the very rare occasions when he is allowed to complete another character's verse line). To attempt to give him verse is to damage Tourneur's conception of the character and its function, and to mar the puritan rhythms of the tallowchandler's rhetoric.

Consequently, although we have tried to restore as verse what, to our minds, Tourneur intended as verse, we have been content to retain as prose rather more than either Nicoll or, especially, Ribner has felt satisfied with.

In accordance with normal New Mermaid practice the Quarto spelling and punctuation have been modernized and additional stage directions supplied, in square brackets, where these seemed to be necessary.

FURTHER READING

Text and Biography
Allardyce Nicoll, ed., *The Works of Cyril Tourneur* (Fanfrolico Press, 1930).
Irving Ribner, *The Atheist's Tragedy* (The Revels Plays, 1964).

Critical Works
Fredson Bowers, *Elizabethan Revenge Tragedy 1587-1642* (Princeton, 1940).
M. C. Bradbrook, *Themes and Conventions of Elizabethan Tragedy* (Cambridge, 1935).
T. S. Eliot, *Selected Essays* (1951)
Una Ellis-Fermor, *The Jacobean Drama* (revised edition, 1961).
David L. Frost, *The School of Shakespeare* (Cambridge, 1968).
L. C. Knights, *Drama and Society in the Age of Jonson* (1937).
P. B. Murray, *A Study of Cyril Tourneur* (Philadelphia, 1964).
Allardyce Nicoll, 'The Revenger's Tragedy and the Virtue of Anonymity', in *Essays on Shakespeare and Elizabethan Drama*, ed. R. Hosley (Columbia, 1963).
R. Ornstein, *The Moral Vision of Jacobean Tragedy* (Madison, Wis., 1960).
J. Peter, *Complaint and Satire in Early English Literature* (Oxford, 1956).
Irving Ribner, *Jacobean Tragedy: The Quest for Moral Order* (1962).
L. G. Salingar, 'The Revenger's Tragedy and the Morality Tradition', in *Scrutiny*, VI (March 1938), and reprinted in *Elizabethan Drama: Modern Essays in Criticism*, ed, R. J. Kaufmann (New York and Oxford, 1961).
S. Schoenbaum, *Internal Evidence and Elizabethan Dramatic Authorship* (1966).
D. P. Walker, *The Decline of Hell* (1964).

and
Nicholas Brooke, *Horrid Laughter* (Open Books, London, 1979).
T. McAlindon, *English Renaissance Tragedy* (Macmillan, 1986).

THE
ATHEIST'S
TRAGEDIE:
OR
The honeſt Man's Reuenge.

As in diuers places it hath often beene Acted.

WRITTEN

By *Cyril Tourneur.*

AT LONDON,
Printed for *Iohn Stepneth*, and *Richard Redmer*, and are to
be ſold at their Shops at the Weſt end of Paules.
1611.

The names and qualities of the Actors

MONTFERRERS, *a Baron*
BELFOREST, *a Baron*
D'AMVILLE, *brother to Montferrers*
LEVIDULCIA, *Lady to Belforest*
CASTABELLA, *daughter to Belforest*
CHARLEMONT, *son to Montferrers*
ROUSARD, *elder son to D'Amville*
SEBASTIAN, *younger son to D'Amville*
LANGUEBEAU SNUFFE, *a Puritan, chaplain to Belforest*
BORACHIO, *D'Amville's instrument*
CATAPLASMA, *a maker of periwigs and attires*
SOQUETTE, *a seeming gentlewoman to Cataplasma*
FRESCO, *servant to Cataplasma*
Other servants
Sergeant in war
Soldiers
Watchmen
Officers
Judges
[*Musketeer*
Doctor
Keeper of the Prison
Executioner]

D'AMVILLE	a combination of English 'vile' with French 'd'ame'
LEVIDULCIA	sweet and light
CASTABELLA	chaste and beautiful
LANGUEBEAU	fine tongue
BORACHIO	drunken
CATAPLASMA	a poultice
FRESCO	fresh

3

THE ATHEIST'S TRAGEDY

Act I, Scene i

Enter D'AMVILLE, BORACHIO, *attended*

D'AMVILLE

I saw my nephew Charlemont but now
Part from his father. Tell him I desire
To speak with him.   *Exit* SERVANT
                    Borachio, thou art read
In Nature and her large philosophy.
Observ'st thou not the very self same course   5
Of revolution both in man and beast?

BORACHIO

The same, for birth, growth, state, decay and death;
Only a man's beholding to his Nature
For th' better composition o' the two.

D'AMVILLE

But where that favour of his Nature is   10

---

3 *read* learned
4 *large* comprehensive
6 *revolution* development
7 *state* maturity
9 *composition* combination
  the two i.e., man and beast
10 *favour* advantage

---

4 *Nature*. With Edmund in *King Lear*, D'Amville would begin his Creed
with 'Thou, Nature, art my goddess'. The word accumulates meanings
as the scene progresses, beginning here as 'the creative and regulative
physical force which is conceived of as operating in the material world
and as the immediate cause of all its phenomena' (OED IV, 11). When
Borachio uses it in 1.8 he has reverted to the word's primary meaning of
the essential qualities or properties of a thing (OED I, 1). A theologian
would answer Borachio's argument (13–16) with the doctrine of Grace.
Grace is contrasted with Nature by Thomas à Kempis in *De Imitatione*
(III, lix, 138): 'Nature sekith to have curious thinges & feire thinges . . .
but grace delitith in simple thinges', and it is this which the Doctor
refers to (though not by name) in V.i, 104ff. It is Divine Grace, residing
in the soul of man, which is 'his being's excellency', and this does not
'yield to Nature's weakness', death. D'Amville's logical deduction, that
'death casts up Our total sum of joy and happiness', is based on a false
premise.

5

> Not full and free, you see a man becomes
> A fool, as little-knowing as a beast.

BORACHIO

> That shows there's nothing in a man above
> His Nature; if there were, consid'ring 'tis
> His being's excellency, 'twould not yield   15
> To Nature's weakness.

D'AMVILLE   Then if death casts up

> Our total sum of joy and happiness,
> Let me have all my senses feasted in
> Th' abundant fulness of delight at once,
> And with a sweet insensible increase   20
> Of pleasing surfeit melt into my dust.

BORACHIO

> That revolution is too short methinks.
> If this life comprehends our happiness,
> How foolish to desire to die so soon!
> And if our time runs home unto the length   25
> Of Nature, how improvident it were
> To spend our substance on a minute's pleasure,
> And after live an age in misery!

D'AMVILLE

> So thou conclud'st that pleasure only flows
> Upon the stream of riches.

BORACHIO   Wealth is lord   30

> Of all felicity.

D'AMVILLE   'Tis oracle,

> For what's a man that's honest without wealth?

BORACHIO

> Both miserable and contemptible.

D'AMVILLE

> He's worse, Borachio. For if charity
> Be an essential part of honesty   35

16 *casts up* reckons up
20 *insensible* imperceptible
23 *comprehends* encloses within its limits
25–6 *runs home unto the length Of Nature* lasts as long as men can expect
31 *oracle* uncontradictable, as though divinely inspired

---

27 *substance*. D'Amville is partly characterized through his frequent use of money-lending terms—'substance', 'principal', 'interest', 'use' (usury); whatever he spends, it is with the intention of getting a good return. Even his attempted seduction of Castabella in IV.iii has a purpose.

And should be practised first upon ourselves,
Which must be granted, then your honest man
That's poor is most dishonest, for he is
Uncharitable to the man whom he
Should most respect. But what doth this touch me,　　40
That seem to have enough? Thanks industry,
'Tis true. Had not my body spread itself
Into posterity perhaps I should
Desire no more increase of substance than
Would hold proportion with mine own dimensions.　　45
Yet even in that sufficiency of state
A man has reason to provide and add,
For what is he hath such a present eye
And so prepared a strength that can foresee
And fortify his substance and himself　　50
Against those accidents, the least whereof
May rob him of an age's husbandry?
And for my children, they are as near to me
As branches to the tree whereon they grow,
And may as numerously be multiplied.　　55
As they increase, so should my providence,
For from my substance they receive the sap
Whereby they live and flourish.
BORACHIO　　　　　　　　　　　Sir, enough.
I understand the mark whereat you aim.

Enter CHARLEMONT

D'AMVILLE
Silence. W'are interrupted. Charlemont!　　60
CHARLEMONT
Good morrow, uncle.

40 *respect* consider
41 *Thanks* Thanks to
46 *sufficiency of state* adequate condition
48 *present* watchful
49 *prepared* ready
52 *husbandry* management

---

56 *providence.* D'Amville is insistent on his providence, understood in the
word's simplest sense of foresight, economy, and provision for the
future. But there is also Divine Providence (whose existence the atheist
of course denies), and the dichotomy between the earthly and the
divine can be felt every time D'Amville uses the word. His final hubristic
boast in V.i, 33ff. juxtaposes the two, and the succeeding irony of
events shows which is the stronger.

D'AMVILLE   Noble Charlemont,
  Good morrow. Is not this the honoured day
  You purposed to set forward to the war?
CHARLEMONT
  My inclination did intend it so.
D'AMVILLE
  And not your resolution?
CHARLEMONT   Yes, my lord,   **65**
  Had not my father contradicted it.
D'AMVILLE
  O noble war, thou first original
  Of all man's honour! How dejectedly
  The baser spirit of our present time
  Hath cast itself below the ancient worth   **70**
  Of our forefathers, from whose noble deeds
  Ignobly we derive our pedigrees.
CHARLEMONT
  Sir, tax not me for his unwillingness.
  By the command of his authority
  My disposition's forced against itself.   **75**
D'AMVILLE
  Nephew, you are the honour of our blood.
  The troop of gentry, whose inferior worth
  Should second your example, are become
  Your leaders; and the scorn of their discourse
  Turns smiling back upon your backwardness.   **80**
CHARLEMONT
  You need not urge my spirit by disgrace;
  'Tis free enough. My father hinders it.
  To curb me, he denies me maintenance
  To put me in the habit of my rank.
  Unbind me from that strong necessity,   **85**
  And call me coward if I stay behind.
D'AMVILLE
  For want of means? Borachio, where's the gold?
  I'd disinherit my posterity
  To purchase honour. 'Tis an interest
  I prize above the principal of wealth.   **90**
  I'm glad I had th' occasion to make known

67 *first original* original cause
82 *free* honourable
84 *habit* equipment
85 *necessity* constraint

How readily my substance shall unlock
Itself to serve you. Here's a thousand crowns.
CHARLEMONT
My worthy uncle, in exchange for this
I leave my bond. So I am doubly bound,   95
By that for the repayment of this gold,
And by this gold to satisfy your love.
D'AMVILLE
Sir, 'tis a witness only of my love,
And love doth always satisfy itself.
Now to your father; labour his consent.   100
My importunity shall second yours.
We will obtain it.
CHARLEMONT   If entreaty fail,
The force of reputation shall prevail.   *Exit*
D'AMVILLE
Go call my sons, that they may take their leaves
Of noble Charlemont. Now, my Borachio!   105
BORACHIO
The substance of our former argument
Was wealth.
D'AMVILLE   The question how to compass it.
BORACHIO
Young Charlemont is going to the war.
D'AMVILLE
O, thou begin'st to take me.
BORACHIO   Mark me then.
Methinks the pregnant wit of man might make   110
The happy absence of this Charlemont
A subject for commodious providence.
He has a wealthy father, ready even
To drop into his grave, and no man's power

95 *doubly bound* i.e., by the legal bond he has just given D'Amville
   and by the family bond
98 *a witness only* no more than a testimony
99 *love doth always satisfy itself* a version of the proverb 'love is its
   own reward' (Tilley L515)
100 *labour* entreat
103 *reputation* opinion, 'what people will think'
107 *compass* attain
109 *take* understand
111 *happy* fortunate
112 *commodious* opportune

115
When Charlemont is gone can interpose
'Twixt you and him.
D'AMVILLE   Th' hast apprehended, both
My meaning and my love. Now let thy trust
For undertaking and for secrecy
Hold measure with thy amplitude of wit,   120
And thy reward shall parallel thy worth.
BORACHIO
My resolution has already bound
Me to your service.
D'AMVILLE   And my heart to thee.

Enter ROUSARD *and* SEBASTIAN

Here are my sons. . . .
There's my eternity. My life in them
And their succession shall for ever live,   125
And in my reason dwells the providence
To add to life as much of happiness.
Let all men lose, so I increase my gain.
I have no feeling of another's pain.   *Exeunt*

[Act I, Scene ii]

Enter old MONTFERRERS *and* CHARLEMONT

MONTFERRERS
I prithee let this current of my tears
Divert thy inclination from the war,
For of my children thou art only left
To promise a succession to my house,
And all the honour thou canst get by arms   5
Will give but vain addition to thy name,
Since from thy ancestors thou dost derive
A dignity sufficient, and as great
As thou hast substance to maintain and bear.
I prithee stay at home.
CHARLEMONT   My noble father,   10
The weakest sigh you breathe hath power to turn
My strongest purpose, and your softest tear
To melt my resolution to as soft

118 *undertaking* enterprise
  3 *art* Collins (are Q)
  6 *vain* meaningless

Obedience. But my affection to the war
Is as hereditary as my blood,   15
To every life of all my ancestry.
Your predecessors were your precedents,
And you are my example. Shall I serve
For nothing but a vain parenthesis
I' th' honoured story of your family,   20
Or hang but like an empty scutcheon
Between the trophies of my predecessors
And the rich arms of my posterity?
There's not a Frenchman of good blood and youth
But either out of spirit or example   25
Is turned a soldier. Only Charlemont
Must be reputed that same heartless thing
That cowards will be bold to play upon.

Enter D'AMVILLE, ROUSARD *and* SEBASTIAN

D'AMVILLE
Good morrow, my lord.
MONTFERRERS
Morrow, good brother.   30
CHARLEMONT
Good morrow, uncle.
D'AMVILLE
Morrow, kind nephew.
What, ha' you washed your eyes wi' tears this morning?
[*To* MONTFERRERS] Come, by my soul, his purpose does
deserve
Your free consent. Your tenderness dissuades him.   35
What to the father of a gentleman
Should be more tender than the maintenance
And the increase of honour to his house?
My lord, here are my boys. I should be proud
That either this were able, or that inclined   40
To be my nephew's brave competitor.

---

14 *affection* disposition; as Charlemont derives his blood from every
 one of his ancestors, so he also derives from them his nature as a
 soldier
21 *scutcheon* escutcheon, a shield with armorial bearing; Charlemont's will be 'empty' if he can win no glory in battle
27 *heartless* with no heart (courage)
41 *competitor* associate

MONTFERRERS
    Your importunities have overcome.
    Pray God my forced grant prove not ominous.
D'AMVILLE [*Aside to* CHARLEMONT]
    We have obtained it.
    [*To* MONTFERRERS] Ominous? In what?
    It cannot be in anything but death,   45
    And I am of a confident belief
    That even the time, place, manner of our deaths
    Do follow fate with that necessity
    That makes us sure to die. And in a thing   50
    Ordained so certainly unalterable
    What can the use of providence prevail?

    [*Enter*] BELFOREST, LEVIDULCIA, [*and*] CASTABELLA, *attended*

BELFOREST
    Morrow, my Lord Montferrers, Lord D'Amville.
    Good morrow, gentlemen. Cousin Charlemont,
    Kindly good morrow. Troth, I was afeared
    I should ha' come too late to tell you that   55
    I wish your undertakings a success
    That may deserve the measure of their worth.
CHARLEMONT
    My lord, my duty would not let me go
    Without receiving your commandments.
BELFOREST
    Accompliments are more for ornament   60
    Than use. We should employ no time in them
    But what our serious business will admit.
MONTFERRERS
    Your favour had by his duty been prevented,
    If we had not withheld him in the way.

---

60 *Accompliments*. 'We have a word now denizened, and brought into
familiar use amongst us, Complement; and for the most part, in an ill
sense; so it is, when the heart of the speaker doth not answer his tongue;
but God forbid but a true heart, and a faire tongue might very well
consist together: As vertue it self receives an addition, by being in a
faire body, so do good intentions of the heart, by being expressed in
faire language'. Donne, Sermon 14 (G. R. Potter and E. M. Simpson,
Donne: Sermons, 10 vols, Berkeley and Los Angeles, 1953, IV, 346–7).
Both Belforest and Charlemont are suspicious of this word ('accom-
pliment' is a variant form of 'compliment'), and at III. i, 49 D'Amville
uses it in Donne's 'ill sense'.

D'AMVILLE
    He was a-coming to present his service.   65
    But now no more. The cook invites to breakfast.
    Will't please your lordship enter? Noble lady!
            [*Exeunt all except*] CHARLEMONT *and* CASTABELLA
CHARLEMONT
    My noble mistress, this accompliment
    Is like an elegant and moving speech
    Composed of many sweet persuasive points   70
    Which second one another with a fluent
    Increase and confirmation of their force,
    Reserving still the best until the last,
    To crown the strong impulsion of the rest
    With a full conquest of the hearer's sense –   75
    Because th' impression of the last we speak
    Doth always longest and most constantly
    Possess the entertainment of remembrance.
    So all that now salute my taking leave
    Have added numerously to the love   80
    Wherewith I did receive their courtesy.
    But you, dear mistress, being the last and best
    That speaks my farewell, like th'imperious close
    Of a most sweet oration, wholly have
    Possessed my liking and shall ever live   85
    Within the soul of my true memory.
    So, mistress, with this kiss I take my leave.
CASTABELLA
    My worthy servant, you mistake th'intent
    Of kissing. 'Twas not meant to separate
    A pair of lovers, but to be the seal   90
    Of love, importing by the joining of
    Our mutual and incorporated breaths
    That we should breathe but one contracted life.
    Or stay at home, or let me go with you.
CHARLEMONT
    My Castabella! For myself to stay   95
    Or you to go would either tax my youth
    With a dishonourable weakness, or
    Your loving purpose with immodesty.

80 *numerously* abundantly
92 *incorporated breaths* the breath which is in each lover's body and
    which, in a kiss, joins the two bodies
93 *contracted* combined and betrothed

Enter LANGUEBEAU SNUFFE

And for the satisfaction of your love,
Here comes a man whose knowledge I have made   100
A witness to the contract of our vows,
Which my return by marriage shall confirm.

LANGUEBEAU SNUFFE
I salute you both with the spirit of copulation. I am already
informed of your matrimonial purposes, and will be a
testimony to the integrity of your promises.   105

CASTABELLA
O the sad trouble of my fearful soul!
My faithful servant! Did you never hear
That when a certain great man went to th'war
The lovely face of Heaven was masked with sorrow,
The sighing winds did move the breast of earth,   110
The heavy clouds hung down their mourning heads
And wept sad showers the day that he went hence,
As if that day presaged some ill success
That fatally should kill his happiness,
And so it came to pass. Methinks my eyes,   115
Sweet Heaven forbid, are like those weeping clouds,
And as their showers presaged, so do my tears,
Some sad event will follow my sad fears.

CHARLEMONT
Fie, superstitious! Is it bad to kiss?

CASTABELLA
May all my fears hurt me no more than this.   [*They kiss*] 120

LANGUEBEAU SNUFFE
Fie, fie, fie, these carnal kisses do stir up the concupiscences
of the flesh.

Enter BELFOREST *and* LEVIDULCIA

LEVIDULCIA
O, here's your daughter under her servant's lips.

CHARLEMONT
Madam, there is no cause you should mistrust
The kiss I gave; 'twas but a parting one.   125

LEVIDULCIA
A lusty blood! Now, by the lip of Love,
Were I to choose, your joining one for me.

BELFOREST
Your father stays to bring you on the way.

114 *fatally* as if ordained by Fate

Farewell. The Great Commander of the war
Prosper the course you undertake. Farewell.   130
CHARLEMONT
My lord, I humbly take my leave. [*To* LEVIDULCIA] Madam,
I kiss your hand. [*To* CASTABELLA] And your sweet lip.
Farewell.
    [*Exeunt all except*] CHARLEMONT *and* LANGUEBEAU [SNUFFE]
Her power to speak is perished in her tears.
Something within me would persuade my stay,   135
But reputation will not yield unto't.
Dear sir, you are the man whose honest trust
My confidence hath chosen for my friend.
I fear my absence will discomfort her.
You have the power and opportunity   140
To moderate her passion. Let her grief
Receive that friendship from you, and your love
Shall not repent itself of courtesy.
LANGUEBEAU
Sir, I want words and protestation to insinuate into your
credit, but in plainness and truth, I will qualify her grief with   145
the spirit of consolation.
CHARLEMONT
Sir, I will take your friendship up at use.
And fear not that your profits shall be small;
Your interest shall exceed your principal.
                                    Exit CHARLEMONT

                Enter D'AMVILLE *and* BORACHIO

D'AMVILLE
Monsieur Languebeau, happily encountered. The honesty of   150
your conversation makes me request more interest in your
familiarity.
LANGUEBEAU
If your lordship will be pleased to salute me without
ceremony, I shall be willing to exchange my service for
your favour, but this worshipping kind of entertainment is a   155
superstitious vanity; in plainness and truth I love it not.
D'AMVILLE
I embrace your disposition and desire to give you as liberal
assurance of my love as my Lord Belforest, your deserved
favourer.

147 *at use* as it were, at usury; i.e., I shall borrow your friendship

LANGUEBEAU
  His lordship is pleased with my plainness and truth of   160
  conversation.
D'AMVILLE
  It cannot displease him. In the behaviour of his noble
  daughter Castabella a man may read her worth and your
  instruction.
LANGUEBEAU
  That gentlewoman is most sweetly modest, fair, honest,   165
  handsome, wise, well-born, and rich.
D'AMVILLE
  You have given me her picture in small.
LANGUEBEAU
  She's like your diamond, a temptation in every man's eye,
  yet not yielding to any light impression herself.
D'AMVILLE
  The praise is hers, but the comparison your own.   170
                                   Gives him the ring

LANGUEBEAU
  You shall forgive me that, sir.
D'AMVILLE
  I will not do so much at your request as forgive you it.
  I will only give you it, sir. By – you will make me swear.
LANGUEBEAU
  O, by no means! Profane not your lips with the foulness of
  that sin. I will rather take it. To save your oath, you shall 175
  lose your ring.– Verily, my lord, my praise came short of her
  worth. She exceeds a jewel. This is but only for ornament,
  she both for ornament and use.
D'AMVILLE
  Yet unprofitably kept without use. She deserves a worthy
  husband, sir. I have often wished a match between my elder   180
  son and her. The marriage would join the houses of Belforest
  and D'Amville into a noble alliance.
LANGUEBEAU
  And the unity of families is a work of love and charity.
D'AMVILLE
  And that work an employment well becoming the goodness of
  your disposition.   185

167 *in small* in miniature, in a few words
169 *light* easy, wanton

LANGUEBEAU

If your lordship please to impose it upon me, I will carry it
without any second end, the surest way to satisfy your wish.

D'AMVILLE

Most joyfully accepted – Rousard! Here are letters to my
Lord Belforest touching my desire to that purpose.

Enter ROUSARD, *sickly*

Rousard, I send you a suitor to Castabella. To this gentle-   190
man's discretion I commit the managing of your suit.
His good success shall be most thankful to your trust.
Follow his instructions; he will be your leader.

LANGUEBEAU

In plainness and truth.

ROUSARD

My leader? Does your lordship think me too weak to give the   195
onset myself?

LANGUEBEAU

I will only assist your proceedings.

ROUSARD

To say true, so I think you had need, for a sick man can
hardly get a woman's good will without help.

LANGUEBEAU

Charlemont, thy gratuity and my promises were both but   200
words, and both like words shall vanish into air.
For thy poor empty hand I must be mute;
This gives me feeling of a better suit.

Exeunt LANGUEBEAU [SNUFFE] *and* ROUSARD

D'AMVILLE

Borachio, didst precisely note this man?

BORACHIO

His own profession would report him pure.   205

D'AMVILLE

And seems to know if any benefit
Arises of religion after death;
Yet but compare's profession with his life;
They so directly contradict themselves
As if the end of his instructions were   210

---

187 *second end* ulterior motive
192 *most thankful to your trust* worth your thanks and your dependence
on him
200 *gratuity* payment
204 *precisely* carefully; but with a play on 'precise' meaning 'puritan'
205 *profession* declared belief

But to divert the world from sin that he
More easily might engross it to himself.
By that I am confirmed an atheist.
Well, Charlemont is gone, and here thou seest
His absence the foundation of my plot.   215

BORACHIO
He is the man whom Castabella loves.

D'AMVILLE
That was the reason I propounded him
Employment fixed upon a foreign place,
To draw his inclination out o' th' way.

BORACHIO
'T has left the passage of our practice free.   220

D'AMVILLE
This Castabella is a wealthy heir,
And by her marriage with my elder son
My house is honoured and my state increased.
This work alone deserves my industry,
But if it prosper, thou shalt see my brain   225
Make this but an induction to a point
So full of profitable policy
That it would make the soul of honesty
Ambitious to turn villain.   I bespeak

BORACHIO
Employment in't. I'll be an instrument   230
To grace performance with dexterity.

D'AMVILLE
Thou shalt. No man shall rob thee of the honour.
Go presently and buy a crimson scarf
Like Charlemont's. Prepare thee a disguise
I'th' habit of a soldier, hurt and lame,   235
And then be ready at the wedding feast,
Where thou shalt have employment in a work
Will please thy disposition.   As I vowed,

BORACHIO
Your instrument shall make your project proud.

212 *engross it* buy it up wholesale
217 *propounded him* proposed to him
223 *state* estate
226 *induction* prologue, preliminary
226 *point* goal
227 *policy* a highly suspect word, associated with Machiavellianism,
      underhand dealing, craftiness, and dishonesty
233 *presently* at once

D'AMVILLE

This marriage will bring wealth. If that succeed,   240
I will increase it though my brother bleed.   *Exeunt*

[Act I, Scene iii]

Enter CASTABELLA, *avoiding the importunity of* ROUSARD

CASTABELLA

Nay, good sir; in troth if you knew how little it pleases me,
you would forbear it.

ROUSARD

I will not leave thee till th'hast entertained me for thy servant.

CASTABELLA

My servant? You are sick, you say. You would tax me of in-
discretion to entertain one that is not able to do me service.   5

ROUSARD

The service of a gentlewoman consists most in chamber
work, and sick men are fittest for the chamber. I prithee give
me a favour.

CASTABELLA

Methinks you have a very sweet favour of your own.

ROUSARD

I lack but your black eye.   10

CASTABELLA

If you go to buffets among the boys, they'll give you one.

ROUSARD

Nay, if you grow bitter, I'll dispraise your black eye.
The gray-eyed morning makes the fairest day.

CASTABELLA

Now that you dissemble not, I could be willing to give you
a favour. What favour would you have?   15

ROUSARD

Any toy, any light thing.

CASTABELLA

Fie! Will you be so uncivil to ask a light thing at a gentlewoman's hand?

---

8 *favour* token of affection; Castabella's reply plays on the meaning
   'appearance'
11 *go to buffets* start fighting
13 *The . . . day* Tilley M1169: 'By the morning one knows the day'
16 *light* trivial: and, in Castabella's reply, wanton

ROUSARD
  Wilt give me a bracelet o' thy hair then?
CASTABELLA   20
  Do you want hair, sir?
ROUSARD
  No, faith, I'll want no hair so long as I can have it for money.
CASTABELLA
  What would you do with my hair then?
ROUSARD
  Wear it for thy sake, sweetheart.
CASTABELLA
  Do you think I love to have my hair worn off?
ROUSARD
  Come, you are so witty now and so sensible.   *Kisses her*   25
CASTABELLA
  Tush, I would I wanted one o'my senses now.
ROUSARD
  Bitter again! What's that? Smelling?
CASTABELLA
  No, no, no. Why now y'are satisfied, I hope. I have given you
  a favour.
ROUSARD
  What favour? A kiss? I prithee give me another.   30
CASTABELLA
  Show me that I gave you then.
ROUSARD
  How should I show it?
CASTABELLA
  You are unworthy of a favour if you will not bestow the
  keeping of it one minute.
ROUSARD
  Well, in plain terms, dost love me? That's the purpose of   35
  my coming.

24 *worn off* It was a common joke that falling hair and baldness were
   caused by venereal disease
25 *sensible* perceptive

19 *bracelet*. The bracelet of hair was a common love-token, whose symbolic
   power is described by Donne in 'The Relique' and again in 'The
   Funerall' where the 'subtile wreath of haire' is seen as his
          outwarde Soule,
       Viceroy to that, which then to heaven being gone,
          Will leave this to controule,
       And keepe these limbes, her Provinces, from dissolution.

CASTABELLA
Love you? Yes, very well.
ROUSARD
Give me thy hand upon't.
CASTABELLA
Nay, you mistake me. If I love you very well, I must not love
you now, for now you are not very well; y'are sick.   40
ROUSARD
This equivocation is for the jest now.
CASTABELLA
I speak't as 'tis now in fashion, in earnest. But I shall not be
in quiet for you, I perceive, till I have given you a favour.
Do you love me?
ROUSARD
With all my heart.   45
CASTABELLA
Then with all my heart I'll give you a jewel to hang in your
ear. Hark ye – I can never love you.   *Exit*
ROUSARD
Call you this a jewel to hang in mine ear? 'Tis no light
favour, for I'll be sworn it comes somewhat heavily to me.
Well, I will not leave her for all this. Methinks it animates a   50
man to stand to't when a woman desires to be rid of him at
the first sight.

[Act I, Scene iv]

Enter BELFOREST *and* LANGUEBEAU SNUFFE

BELFOREST
I entertain the offer of this match
With purpose to confirm it presently.
I have already moved it to my daughter.
Her soft excuses savoured at the first,
Methought, but of a modest innocence   5
Of blood, whose unmoved stream was never drawn
Into the current of affection. But when I

---

43 *in quiet for you* left in peace by you
51 *stand to* persist; also with the bawdy sense of the Porter in
     Macbeth: 'much drink may be said to be an equivocator with
     lechery: it . . . makes him stand to, and not stand to' (II.iii, 31ff.)
3 *moved* proposed
7 *affection* emotion

Replied with more familiar arguments,
Thinking to make her apprehension bold,
Her modest blush fell to a pale dislike, 10
And she refused it with such confidence
As if she had been prompted by a love
Inclining firmly to some other man,
And in that obstinacy she remains.

LANGUEBEAU
Verily, that disobedience doth not become a child. It pro- 15
ceedeth from an unsanctified liberty. You will be accessory to
your own dishonour if you suffer it.

BELFOREST
Your honest wisdom has advised me well.
Once more I'll move her by persuasive means.
If she resist, all mildness set apart, 20
I will make use of my authority.

LANGUEBEAU
And instantly, lest fearing your constraint her contrary
affection teach her some device that may prevent you.

BELFOREST
To cut off every opportunity
Procrastination may assist her with, 25
This instant night she shall be married.

LANGUEBEAU   Best.

Enter CASTABELLA

CASTABELLA
Please it your lordship, my mother attends
I'th'gallery and desires your conference.   *Exit* BELFOREST
This means I used to bring me to your ear.
Time cuts off circumstance; I must be brief. 30
To your integrity did Charlemont
Commit the contract of his love and mine,
Which now so strong a hand seeks to divide
That if your grave advice assist me not,
I shall be forced to violate my faith. 35

LANGUEBEAU
Can he deserve your love who, in neglect of your delightful
conversation and in obstinate contempt of all your prayers

8 *familiar* intimate
9 *apprehension* understanding
22 *contrary affection* the love that opposes her father's will
30 *Time cuts off circumstance* there is no time for formality

and tears, absents himself so far from your sweet fellowship,
and with a purpose so contracted to that absence that you
see he purchases your separation with the hazard of his blood   40
and life, fearing to want pretence to part your companies?
'Tis rather hate that doth division move;
Love still desires the presence of his love.
Verily, he is not of the Family of Love.

CASTABELLA

O do not wrong him. 'Tis a generous mind   45
That led his disposition to the war,
For gentle love and noble courage are
So near allied that one begets another,
Or love is sister, and courage is the brother.
Could I affect him better than before,   50
His soldier's heart would make me love him more.

LANGUEBEAU

But, Castabella –

Enter LEVIDULCIA

LEVIDULCIA

Tush, you mistake the way into a woman;
The passage lies not through her reason but her blood.

Exit LANGUEBEAU [SNUFFE], CASTABELLA *about to follow*

Nay, stay! How wouldst thou call the child   55
That being raised with cost and tenderness
To full ability of body and means
Denies relief unto the parents who
Bestowed that bringing up?

---

39 *contracted to* determined upon
41 *fearing to want pretence* afraid that he will not have an excuse
50 *affect* love

---

44 *the Family of Love.* This religious sect, originating in Holland in the
   middle of the sixteenth century, gained popularity, notoriety, and
   ridicule in England. Its professions were puritan, but its members,
   claiming to believe that love was more important than theology, were
   accused of being more earthly than divine in their love. Mistress Purge
   in Middleton's *The Family of Love* (1607) gives a good account of the
   Family to two would-be converts: 'you must never hereafter frequent
   taverns nor tap-houses, no masques nor mummeries, no pastimes nor
   playhouses . . . During the light of the candle you are to be very atten-
   tive; which being extinguished, how to behave yourselves I will deliver
   in private' (IV.i).
50–1 Castabella shows her true magnanimity in this adumbration of Love-
   lace's 'I could not love thee (Deare) so much, Lov'd I not Honour
   more'.

CASTABELLA   Unnatural.

LEVIDULCIA
   Then Castabella is unnatural.   60
   Nature, the loving mother of us all,
   Brought forth a woman for her own relief,
   By generation to revive her age,
   Which, now thou hast ability and means
   Presented, most unkindly dost deny.   65

CASTABELLA
   Believe me, mother, I do love a man.

LEVIDULCIA
   Preferest th'affection of an absent love
   Before the sweet possession of a man,
   The barren mind before the fruitful body,
   Where our creation has no reference   70
   To man but in his body, being made
   Only for generation which (unless
   Our children can be gotten by conceit)
   Must from the body come. If reason were
   Our counsellor, we would neglect the work   75
   Of generation for the prodigal
   Expense it draws us to of that which is
   The wealth of life. Wise Nature, therefore, hath
   Reserved for an inducement to our sense
   Our greatest pleasure in that greatest work,   80
   Which being offered thee, thy ignorance
   Refuses for th'imaginary joy
   Of an unsatisfied affection to
   An absent man – whose blood once spent i'th'war,
   Then he'll come home sick, lame, and impotent,   85

62 *relief* assistance
63 *generation* breeding
63 *her age* i.e., Nature's age; the idea was prevalent that the world
   was growing old, the best was past
65 *unkindly* unnaturally
70 *Where* Whereas
73 *conceit* imagination

76–8 *the prodigal . . . life.* Ribner quotes Donne's 'Farewell to Love' in
   which the poet alludes to the popular belief that sexual intercourse
   shortened life: 'each such Act, they say, Diminisheth the length of life
   a day'. The 'wealth of life' is spirit, understood both as the vital spirits
   infusing the whole body and, more narrowly, as the seminal fluid (as in
   Shakespeare's Sonnet 129, 'Th'expence of Spirit in a waste of shame
   Is lust in action').

And wed thee to a torment, like the pain
Of Tantalus, continuing thy desire
With fruitless presentation of the thing
It loves, still moved and still unsatisfied.

Enter BELFOREST, D'AMVILLE, ROUSARD, SEBASTIAN, LANGUEBEAU
[SNUFFE, *and others*]

BELFOREST
  Now, Levidulcia, hast thou yet prepared   90
  My daughter's love to entertain this man,
  Her husband here?
LEVIDULCIA   I'm but her mother i'law;
  Yet if she were my very flesh and blood,
  I could advise no better for her good.
ROUSARD
  Sweet wife! Thy joyful husband thus salutes   95
  Thy cheek.
CASTABELLA   My husband? O, I am betrayed.
  [*To* LANGUEBEAU SNUFFE] Dear friend of Charlemont, your
  purity
  Professes a divine contempt o'th' world;
  O be not bribed by that you so neglect,
  In being the world's hated instrument,   100
  To bring a just neglect upon yourself.
                 Kneel[*s*] *from one to another*
  [*To* BELFOREST] Dear father, let me but examine my
  Affection. [*To* D'AMVILLE] Sir, your prudent judgement can
  Persuade your son that 'tis improvident
  To marry one whose disposition he   105
  Did ne'er observe. [*To* ROUSARD] Good sir, I may be of
  A nature so unpleasing to your mind,
  Perhaps you'll curse the fatal hour wherein
  You rashly married me.
D'AMVILLE   My Lord Belforest,
  I would not have her forced against her choice.   110
BELFOREST
  Passion o' me, thou peevish girl. I charge

87 *Tantalus* as a punishment for his tale-bearing, Tantalus was
   condemned in Hades to stand waist-deep in water and always
   thirst, and be constantly offered fruit which he could never grasp
89 *moved* aroused
92 *mother i'law* stepmother
94 *for her good* Collins (for good Q)
101 *neglect* scorn

Thee by my blessing and th'authority
I have to claim th'obedience, marry him.

CASTABELLA

Now Charlemont! O my presaging tears,
This sad event hath followed my sad fears.   115

SEBASTIAN

A rape, a rape, a rape!

BELFOREST

How now?

D'AMVILLE

What's that?

SEBASTIAN

Why what is't but a rape to force a wench to marry, since
it forces her to lie with him she would not?   120

LANGUEBEAU

Verily, his tongue is an unsanctified member.

SEBASTIAN

Verily, your gravity becomes your perished soul as hoary
mouldiness does rotten fruit.

BELFOREST

Cousin, y'are both uncivil and profane.

D'AMVILLE

Thou disobedient villain, get thee out of my sight.   125
Now, by my soul, I'll plague thee for this rudeness.

BELFOREST

Come, set forward to the church.

Exeunt [all except] SEBASTIAN

SEBASTIAN

And verify the proverb – the nearer the church, the further
from God. Poor wench, for thy sake may his ability die in his
appetite, that thou beest not troubled with him thou lovest   130
not. May his appetite move thy desire to another man, so he
shall help to make himself cuckold. And let that man be one
that he pays wages to, so thou shalt profit by him thou hatest.
Let the chambers be matted, the hinges oiled, the curtain
rings silenced, and the chamber-maid hold her peace at his   135
own request, that he may sleep the quietlier; and in that
sleep let him be soundly cuckolded. And when he knows it
and seeks to sue a divorce, let him have no other satisfaction

128 *the nearer . . . God* Tilley C380
129 *ability* i.e., sexual ability
134 *matted* covered with rushes
134 *curtain rings* i.e., on the bed-posts
138 *satisfaction* i.e., in law

than this: *he lay by and slept; the law will take no hold of her*
because he winked at it. 140

Exit

Act II, Scene i

Music. A banquet. In the night. Enter D'AMVILLE, BELFOREST,
LEVIDULCIA, ROUSARD, CASTABELLA, LANGUEBEAU SNUFFE *at one*
door; at the other door CATAPLASMA *and* SOQUETTE, *ushered*
by FRESCO

LEVIDULCIA

Mistress Cataplasma, I expected you an hour since.

CATAPLASMA

Certain ladies at my house, madam, detained me; otherwise
I had attended your ladyship sooner.

LEVIDULCIA

We are beholding to you for your company. My lord, I pray
you bid these gentlewomen welcome; th'are my invited 5
friends.

D'AMVILLE

Gentlewomen, y'are welcome; pray sit down.

LEVIDULCIA

Fresco, by my Lord D'Amville's leave I prithee go into the
buttery. Thou sha't find some o' my men there; if they bid
thee not welcome, they are very loggerheads. 10

FRESCO

If your loggerheads will not, your hogsheads shall, madam,
if I get into the buttery. *Exit*

D'AMVILLE

That fellow's disposition to mirth should be our present
example. Let's be grave and meditate when our affairs require
our seriousness. 'Tis out of season to be heavily disposed. 15

LEVIDULCIA

We should be all wound up into the key of mirth.

D'AMVILLE

The music there!

BELFOREST

Where's my Lord Montferrers? Tell him here's a room
attends him.

140 *winked* connived
  10 *loggerheads* clowns; a reference to 'loggerheads' is usually followed
  in Elizabethan-Jacobean drama by a mention of 'hogsheads'; cf.
  1 Henry IV, 'With three or four loggerheads, amongst three or
  fourscore hogsheads'. (II.iv, 4–5)

Enter MONTFERRERS

MONTFERRERS
　Heaven give your marriage that I am deprived of, joy.　　　20
D'AMVILLE
　My Lord Belforest, Castabella's health!

　　　　　　　　　　　　D'AMVILLE *drinks*

　Set ope the cellar doors, and let this health
　Go freely round the house. – Another to
　Your son, my lord, to noble Charlemont.
　He is a soldier. Let the instruments　　　　　　　　　　25
　Of war congratulate his memory.　　*Drums and trumpets*

Enter a SERVANT

SERVANT
　My lord, here's one i'th'habit of a soldier says he is newly
　returned from Ostend and has some business of import to
　speak.
D'AMVILLE
　Ostend! Let him come in. My soul foretells　　　　　30
　He brings the news will make our music full.
　My brother's joy would do't, and here comes he
　Will raise it.

Enter BORACHIO *disguised*

MONTFERRERS　O my spirit, it does dissuade
　My tongue to question him, as if it knew
　His answer would displease.
D'AMVILLE　　　　　　　Soldier, what news?　　　35
　We heard a rumour of a blow you gave
　The enemy.
BORACHIO　　　'Tis very true, my lord.
BELFOREST
　Canst thou relate it?
BORACHIO　　　　　Yes.
D'AMVILLE　　　　　　　I prithee do.
BORACHIO
　The enemy, defeated of a fair
　Advantage by a flattering stratagem,　　　　　　　40

21–6　*My . . . memory* as prose Q
　26　*congratulate* celebrate
　28　*Ostend* the siege of Ostend began in 1601 and was lifted in 1604
　30–8　*Ostend . . . do* as prose Q
　31　*make our music full* complete our happiness
　40　*flattering* deceptive

Plants all th'artillery against the town,
Whose thunder and lightning made our bulwarks shake,
And threatened in that terrible report
The storm wherewith they meant to second it.
Th'assault was general, but for the place   45
That promised most advantage to be forced,
The pride of all their army was drawn forth
And equally divided into front
And rear. They marched, and coming to a stand,
Ready to pass our channel at an ebb,   50
W'advised it for our safest course to draw
Our sluices up and make't unpassable.
Our governor opposed and suffered 'em
To charge us home e'en to the rampier's foot,
But when their front was forcing up our breach   55
At push o'pike, then did his policy
Let go the sluices and tripped up the heels
Of the whole body of their troop that stood
Within the violent current of the stream.
Their front, beleaguered 'twixt the water and   60
The town, seeing the flood was grown too deep
To promise them a safe retreat, exposed
The force of all their spirits, like the last
Expiring gasp of a strong-hearted man,
Upon the hazard of one charge, but were   65
Oppressed and fell. The rest that could not swim
Were only drowned, but those that thought to 'scape
By swimming were by murderers that flankered
The level of the flood both drowned and slain.

D'AMVILLE
Now by my soul, soldier, a brave service.   70

MONTFERRERS
O what became of my dear Charlemont?

BORACHIO
Walking next day upon the fatal shore,
Among the slaughtered bodies of their men
Which the full-stomached sea had cast upon
The sands, it was m'unhappy chance to light   75
Upon a face, whose favour when it lived

56 *push o'pike* hand-to-hand combat
68 *flankered* protected the sides (flanks) of the channel
76 *favour* features

My astonished mind informed me I had seen.
He lay in's armour as if that had been
His coffin, and the weeping sea, like one
Whose milder temper doth lament the death   80
Of him whom in his rage he slew, runs up
The shore, embraces him, kisses his cheek,
Goes back again, and forces up the sands
To bury him, and every time it parts
Sheds tears upon him, till at last, as if   85
It could no longer endure to see the man
Whom it had slain, yet loath to leave him, with
A kind of unresolved unwilling pace,
Winding her waves one in another, like
A man that folds his arms or wrings his hands   90
For grief, ebbed from the body and descends,
As if it would sink down into the earth
And hide itself for shame of such a deed.

D'AMVILLE
And, soldier, who was this?
MONTFERRERS   O Charlemont!

BORACHIO
Your fear hath told you that whereof my grief   95
Was loath to be the messenger.
CASTABELLA   O God.   *Exit* CASTABELLA

D'AMVILLE
Charlemont drowned? Why how could that be, since
It was the adverse party that received
The overthrow?

BORACHIO
His forward spirit pressed into the front,   100
And being engaged within the enemy
When they retreated through the rising stream,
I'th' violent confusion of the throng
Was overborne and perished in the flood.
And here's the sad remembrance of his life,   105
                    [*He shows*] *the scarf*
Which for his sake I will for ever wear.

MONTFERRERS
Torment me not with witnesses of that
Which I desire not to believe, yet must.

97–9 *Charlemont . . . overthrow* as prose Q
98 *adverse* enemy

D'AMVILLE

   Thou art a screech-owl and dost come i'night
   To be the cursed messenger of death.   110
   Away. Depart my house, or, by my soul,
   You'll find me a more fatal enemy
   Than ever was Ostend. Be gone. Dispatch.

BORACHIO

   Sir, 'twas my love –

D'AMVILLE   Your love to vex my heart
   With that I hate? Hark, do you hear, you knave?   115
   [*Aside to* BORACHIO] O th'art a most delicate sweet eloquent
                                villain.

BORACHIO [*Aside to* D'AMVILLE]

   Was't not well counterfeited?

D'AMVILLE [*Aside to* BORACHIO]

   Rarely. [*Aloud*] Be gone; I will not here reply.

BORACHIO

   Why then, farewell. I will not trouble you.   *Exit*

D'AMVILLE [*Aside*]

   So. The foundation's laid. Now by degrees   120
   The work will rise and soon be perfected.
   [*To the others*] O this uncertain state of mortal man!

BELFOREST

   What then? It is th'inevitable fate
   Of all things underneath the moon.

D'AMVILLE   'Tis true.
   Brother, for health's sake overcome your grief.   125

MONTFERRERS

   I cannot sir. I am uncapable
   Of comfort. My turn will be next. I feel
   Myself not well.

D'AMVILLE   You yield too much to grief.

LANGUEBEAU

   All men are mortal. The hour of death is uncertain. Age
   makes sickness the more dangerous, and grief is subject to   130

130 *subject to distraction* likely to turn to madness

---

109 *screech-owl*. This bird was popularly regarded as a creature of ill-omen
   and the harbinger of death; cf. Webster, *The Duchess of Malfi*: 'The
   screech owl and the whistler shrill Call upon our Dame, aloud, And bid
   her quickly don her shroud' (IV.ii, 176–8).

124 *underneath the moon*. It was held that all creatures beneath the moon,
   the nearest of the planets to the earth in the Ptolemaic (geocentric)
   universe, were subject to decay and mutability; above the moon there
   was permanence and immortality.

distraction. You know not how soon you may be deprived
of the benefit of sense. In my understanding, therefore, you
shall do well if you be sick to set your state in present order.
Make your will.

D'AMVILLE [*Aside*]
I have my wish.
[*To the others*] Lights for my brother.

MONTFERRERS   I'll withdraw a while, 135
And crave the honest counsel of this man.

BELFOREST
With all my heart. I pray attend him, sir.
                  Exeunt MONTFERRERS *and* [LANGUEBEAU] SNUFFE
This next room, please your lordship.

D'AMVILLE   Where you will.
                  Exeunt BELFOREST *and* D'AMVILLE

LEVIDULCIA
My daughter's gone. Come son. Mistress Cataplasma, come;
we'll up into her chamber. I'd fain see how she entertains 140
the expectation of her husband's bedfellowship.

ROUSARD
'Faith, howsoever she entertains it, I
Shall hardly please her; therefore let her rest.

LEVIDULCIA
Nay, please her hardly, and you please her best.
                                  Exeunt

[Act II, Scene ii]

Enter three SERVANTS, *drunk, drawing in* FRESCO

1ST SERVANT
Boy! Fill some drink, boy.

FRESCO
Enough, good sir; not a drop more by this light.

2ND SERVANT
Not by this light? Why then put out the candles, and
we'll drink i' th' dark and t'wou't, old boy.

142–3 *'Faith . . . rest* as prose Q
144 *please her hardly* Levidulcia transposes the words of Rousard's
    preceding line to construct the opposite of his meaning.
  4 *and* if
    t'wou't thou wilt

131–2 *deprived . . . sense.* To this day, a will must affirm that the testator is
    'in sound mind'.

FRESCO

  No, no, no, no, no. 5

3RD SERVANT

  Why then take thy liquor. A health, Fresco! *Kneel*[s]

FRESCO

  Your health will make me sick, sir.

1ST SERVANT

  Then 'twill bring you o' your knees I hope, sir.

FRESCO

  May I not stand and pledge it, sir?

2ND SERVANT

  I hope you will do as we do. 10

FRESCO

  Nay then, indeed I must not stand, for you cannot.

3RD SERVANT

  Well said, old boy.

FRESCO

  Old boy! You'll make me a young child anon, for if I continue
  this, I shall scarce be able to go alone.

1ST SERVANT

  My body is as weak as water, Fresco. 15

FRESCO

  Good reason, sir. The beer has sent all the malt up into your
  brain and left nothing but the water in your body.

Enter D'AMVILLE *and* BORACHIO, *closely observing their*
drunkenness

D'AMVILLE

  Borachio, seest those fellows?

BORACHIO Yes, my lord.

D'AMVILLE

  Their drunkenness that seems ridiculous
  Shall be a serious instrument to bring 20
  Our sober purposes to their success.

BORACHIO

  I am prepared for th'execution, sir.

---

9 *pledge it* drink a toast
14 *to go* to walk

---

6 s.d. *Kneel*[s]. Ribner points out that it was the custom for London
gallants to kneel when toasting their mistresses, after which they were
dubbed 'knights': he quotes *A Yorkshire Tragedy* (1608): 'they call it
knighting in London, when they drink upon their knees' (Sig. A3ᵛ).

D'AMVILLE
Cast off this habit and about it straight.
BORACHIO
Let them drink healths and drown their brains i' the flood;
I'll promise them they shall be pledged in blood.   *Exit*   25
1ST SERVANT
You ha' left a damnable snuff here.
2ND SERVANT
Do you take that in snuff, sir?
1ST SERVANT
You are a damnable rogue then.
                    [*They fight and fall*] *together by th'ears*
D'AMVILLE [*Aside*]
Fortune, I honour thee. My plot still rises
According to the model of mine own desires.   30
[*To the others*] Lights for my brother! What, ha' you drunk
yourselves mad, you knaves.
[1ST SERVANT]
My lord, the jacks abused me.
D'AMVILLE
I think they are the jacks indeed that have abused thee.
Dost hear? That fellow is a proud knave. He has abused   35
thee. As thou goest over the fields by and by in lighting
my brother home, I'll tell thee what sha't do: knock him
over the pate with thy torch; I'll bear thee out in't.
1ST SERVANT
I will singe the goose by this torch.   *Exit*
D'AMVILLE [*to the* 2ND SERVANT]
Dost hear, fellow? Seest thou that proud knave? I have given   40
him a lesson for his sauciness. 'Has wronged thee. I'll tell
thee what sha't do: as we go over the fields by and by, clap
him suddenly o'er the coxcomb with thy torch; I'll bear
thee out in't.
2ND SERVANT
I will make him understand as much.   *Exit*   45

---

26 *snuff* dregs; OED quotes an early seventeenth-century source
   saying that 'to leave a little snuffe Is petty treason'
27 *take . . . in snuff* take offence at
33 *jacks* a synonym for knaves and also, as D'Amville uses it in the
   next line, a name for vessels for liquor, either for holding it or for
   drinking from
38 *bear thee out* give you my support
43 *coxcomb* head (originally a fool's cap)

Enter LANGUEBEAU SNUFFE

D'AMVILLE

Now, Monsieur Snuffe, what has my brother done?

LANGUEBEAU

Made his will, and by that will made you his heir, with this
proviso, that as occasion shall hereafter move him, he may
revoke or alter it when he pleases.

D'AMVILLE

Yes, let him if he can. [*Aside*] – I'll make it sure   50
From his revoking.

Enter MONTFERRERS *and* BELFOREST, *attended with lights*

MONTFERRERS   Brother, now good night.

D'AMVILLE

The sky is dark; we'll bring you o'er the fields.
[*Aside*] Who can but strike wants wisdom to maintain;
He that strikes safe and sure has heart and brain.

                                        Exeunt

[Act II, Scene iii]

Enter CASTABELLA *alone*

CASTABELLA

O love, thou chaste affection of the soul,
Without th'adult'rate mixture of the blood,
That virtue which to goodness addeth good,
The minion of Heaven's heart. Heaven, is't my fate
For loving that thou lov'st, to get thy hate?   5
Or was my Charlemont thy chosen love,
And therefore hast received him to thyself?
Then I confess thy anger's not unjust:
I was thy rival. Yet to be divorced
From love has been a punishment enough,   10
Sweet Heaven, without being married unto hate.
Hadst thou been pleased – O double misery!
Yet since thy pleasure hath inflicted it,
If not my heart, my duty shall submit.

Enter LEVIDULCIA, ROUSARD, CATAPLASMA, SOQUETTE, *and* FRESCO,
                    with a lantern

LEVIDULCIA

Mistress Cataplasma, good night. I pray when your man   15

53 *maintain* persist
4 *minion* favourite

has brought you home, let him return and light me to my
house.
CATAPLASMA
He shall instantly wait on your ladyship.
LEVIDULCIA
Good, Mistress Cataplasma, for my servants are all drunk;
I cannot be beholding to 'em for their attendance.   20
                    Exeunt CATAPLASMA, SOQUETTE *and* FRESCO
O here's your bride.
ROUSARD   And melancholic too,
Methinks.
LEVIDULCIA
          How can she choose? Your sickness will
Distaste th'expected sweetness o' the night.
That makes her heavy.
ROUSARD   That should make her light.
LEVIDULCIA
Look you to that.
CASTABELLA   What sweetness speak you of?   25
The sweetness of the night consists in rest.
ROUSARD
With that sweetness thou shalt be surely blest
Unless my groaning wake thee. Do not moan.
LEVIDULCIA
Sh'had rather you would wake and make her groan.
ROUSARD
Nay 'troth, sweetheart, I will not trouble thee.   30
Thou shalt not lose thy maidenhead tonight.
CASTABELLA
O might that weakness ever be in force,
I never would desire to sue divorce.
ROUSARD
Wilt go to bed?
CASTABELLA   I will attend you, sir.
ROUSARD
Mother, good night.
LEVIDULCIA   Pleasure be your bedfellow.   35
                    Exeunt ROUSARD *and* CASTABELLA
Why sure their generation was asleep
When she begot those dormice, that she made

23 *Distaste* Spoil
24 *heavy* sad
36 *their generation was asleep* their parents could not have been
   awake when they were conceived

Them up so weakly and imperfectly.
One wants desire, the t'other ability –
When my affection even with their cold bloods,   40
As snow rubbed through an active hand does make
The flesh to burn, by agitation is
Inflamed! I could unbrace and entertain
The air to cool it.

Enter SEBASTIAN

SEBASTIAN   That but mitigates
The heat; rather embrace and entertain   45
A younger brother; he can quench the fire.
LEVIDULCIA
Can you so, sir? Now I beshrew your ear.
Why, bold Sebastian, how dare you approach
So near the presence of your displeased father?
SEBASTIAN
Under the protection of his present absence.   50
LEVIDULCIA
Belike you knew he was abroad then?
SEBASTIAN   Yes.
Let me encounter you so; I'll persuade
Your means to reconcile me to his love.
LEVIDULCIA
Is that the way? I understand you not.
But for your reconcilement, meet m'at home;   55
I'll satisfy your suit.
SEBASTIAN   Within this half hour.

Exit SEBASTIAN

LEVIDULCIA
Or within this whole hour. When you will – A lusty blood!
Has both the presence and the spirit of a man. I like the
freedom of his behaviour. Ho! Sebastian! Gone? Has set
my blood a-boiling i' my veins, and now, like water poured   60
upon the ground that mixes itself with every moisture it
meets, I could clasp with any man.

Enter FRESCO *with a lantern*

O Fresco, art thou come?
If t'other fail, then thou art entertained.

40 *affection* passion, lust
43 *unbrace* undress
47 *your ear* i.e., for having overheard her

Lust is a spirit which whosoe'er doth raise,   65
The next man that encounters boldly lays.   *Exeunt*

[Act II, Scene iv]

Enter BORACHIO *warily and hastily over the stage, with a stone
in either hand*

BORACHIO
Such stones men use to raise a house upon,
But with these stones I go to ruin one.

Descends

Enter two SERVANTS, *drunk, fighting with their torches;* D'AMVILLE,
MONTFERRERS, BELFOREST *and* LANGUEBEAU SNUFFE

BELFOREST
Passion o'me, you drunken knaves, you'll put
The lights out.
D'AMVILLE   No, my lord, th'are but in jest.
1ST SERVANT
Mine's out.   5
D'AMVILLE
Then light it at his head; that's light enough.
'Fore God, th'are out. You drunken rascals, back
And light 'em.
BELFOREST   'Tis exceeding dark.   *Exeunt* SERVANTS
D'AMVILLE   No matter;
I am acquainted with the way. Your hand.
Let's easily walk. I'll lead you till they come.   10
MONTFERRERS
My soul's oppressed with grief. 'T lies heavy at
My heart. O my departed son, ere long
I shall be with thee.
               D'AMVILLE *thrusts him down into the gravel pit*
D'AMVILLE   Marry, God forbid!
MONTFERRERS
O, O, O.

---

65 *spirit* there is a double pun here (with 'lays' in the next line) on
   the ghost which must be laid (= exorcized) and the sexual desire
   which must be satisfied
2 s.d. *Descends* having crossed from one side of the stage to the
   other, Borachio now climbs down from the platform and the
   place where he waits becomes the 'gravel pit'
3–98 *Passion . . . perished* as prose Q

D'AMVILLE
  Now all the host of heaven forbid! Knaves! Rogues!   15
BELFOREST
  Pray God he be not hurt! He's fall'n into the gravel pit.
D'AMVILLE
  Brother, dear brother! Rascals, villains, knaves!

          Enter the SERVANTS *with lights*

  Eternal darkness damn you; come away.
  Go round about into the gravel pit,
  And help my brother up. [*Exeunt* SERVANTS] Why what a
                                        strange   20
  Unlucky night is this! Is't not, my lord?
  I think that dog that howled the news of grief,
  That fatal screech-owl, ushered on this mischief.

          Enter [SERVANTS] *with the murdered body*

LANGUEBEAU
  Mischief indeed, my lord. Your brother's dead.
BELFOREST
  He's dead.
1ST SERVANT
          He's dead.
D'AMVILLE   Dead be your tongues! Drop out   25
  Mine eye-balls, and let envious Fortune play
  At tennis with 'em. Have I lived to this?
  Malicious Nature! Hadst thou born me blind,
  Th'hadst yet been something favourable to me.
  No breath? No motion? Prithee tell me, Heaven,   30
  Hast shut thine eye to wink at murder, or
  Hast put this sable garment on to mourn
  At's death?
  Not one poor spark in the whole spacious sky
  Of all that endless number would vouchsafe   35
  To shine? You viceroys to the king of Nature!
  Whose constellations govern mortal births,
  Where is that fatal planet ruled at his
  Nativity? That might ha' pleased to light
  Him out, as well into th'world, unless   40
  It be ashamed t'have been the instrument
  Of such a good man's cursed destiny.

  26–7 *play At tennis.* A Renaissance commonplace; cf. Webster, *The
     Duchess of Malfi*: 'We are merely the stars' tennis-balls, struck and
     banded Which way please them'.

BELFOREST
    Passion transports you. Recollect yourself.
    Lament him not. Whether our deaths be good
    Or bad, it is not death but life that tries.   45
    He lived well, therefore questionless well dies.
D'AMVILLE
    Ay, 'tis an easy thing for him that has
    No pain to talk of patience. Do you think
    That Nature has no feeling?
BELFOREST   Feeling? Yes.
    But has she purposed anything for nothing?   50
    What good receives this body by your grief?
    Whether is't more unnatural not to grieve
    For him you cannot help with it, or hurt
    Yourself with grieving and yet grieve in vain?
D'AMVILLE
    Indeed, had he been taken from me like   55
    A piece o' dead flesh, I should neither ha' felt it
    Nor grieved for 't. But come hither, pray look here.
    Behold the lively tincture of his blood!
    Neither the dropsy nor the jaundice in't,
    But the true freshness of a sanguine red,   60
    For all the fog of this black murd'rous night
    Has mixed with it. For anything I know,
    He might ha' lived till doomsday and ha' done
    More good than either you or I. O brother!
    He was a man of such a native goodness,   65
    As if regeneration had been given
    Him in his mother's womb; so harmless
    That rather than ha' trod upon a worm
    He would ha' shunned the way; so dearly pitiful
    That ere the poor could ask his charity   70
    With dry eyes, he gave 'em relief wi' tears –
    With tears – yes, faith, with tears.
BELFOREST   Take up the corpse.
    For wisdom's sake, let reason fortify
    This weakness.
D'AMVILLE   Why, what would you ha' me do?
    Foolish Nature will have her course in spite   75
    O' wisdom. But I have e'en done.
    All these words were but a great wind, and now

45 *tries* tests
66–7 *As . . . womb* i.e., as though he had been redeemed from original
    sin before he was even born

This shower of tears has laid it, I am calm
Again. You may set forward when you will.
I'll follow you like one that must and would not.   80
LANGUEBEAU
Our opposition will but trouble him.
BELFOREST
The grief that melts to tears by itself is spent;
Passion resisted grows more violent.
                    Exeunt [all except] D'AMVILLE. BORACHIO *ascends*
D'AMVILLE
Here's a sweet comedy. 'T begins with *O Dolentis* and con-
cludes with ha, ha, he.   85
BORACHIO
Ha, ha, he.
D'AMVILLE   O my echo! I could stand
Reverberating this sweet musical air
Of joy till I had perished my sound lungs
With violent laughter. Lovely night-raven!
Th'hast seized a carcass.
BORACHIO   Put him out on's pain.   90
I lay so fitly underneath the bank
From whence he fell, that ere his faltering tongue
Could utter double O, I knocked out's brains
With this fair ruby, and had another stone
Just of this form and bigness ready; that   95
I laid i' th' broken skull upo' the ground
For's pillow, against the which they thought he fell
And perished.
D'AMVILLE
Upon this ground I'll build my manor house,
And this shall be the chiefest corner-stone.   100
BORACHIO
'T has crowned the most judicious murder that
The brain of man was e'er delivered of.
D'AMVILLE
Ay, mark the plot. Not any circumstance
That stood within the reach of the design

---

94 *ruby* i.e., because the stone was red with Montferrers's blood

---

84 *a sweet comedy*. D'Amville's definition of comedy is the medieval one,
to be found in Lydgate's *Troy Book*: 'A comedie hath in his gynnyng,
At prima face, a maner compleynyng, And afterward endeth in gladnes'
(ii. 847–9).

Of persons, dispositions, matter, time,   105
Or place, but by this brain of mine was made
An instrumental help, yet nothing from
Th'induction to th'accomplishment seemed forced
Or done o' purpose, but by accident.

BORACHIO
First my report that Charlemont was dead,   110
Though false, yet covered with a mask of truth.

D'AMVILLE
Ay, and delivered in as fit a time,
When all our minds so wholly were possessed
With one affair, that no man would suspect
A thought employed for any second end.   115

BORACHIO
Then the precisian to be ready when
Your brother spake of death, to move his will.

D'AMVILLE
His business called him thither, and it fell
Within his office, unrequested to't.
From him it came religiously and saved   120
Our project from suspicion, which if I
Had moved had been endangered.   Then your healths,

BORACHIO
Though seeming but the ordinary rites
And ceremonies due to festivals –

D'AMVILLE
Yet used by me to make the servants drunk,   125
An instrument the plot could not have missed.
'Twas easy to set drunkards by the ears;
Th'had nothing but their torches to fight with,
And when those lights were out –   Then darkness did

BORACHIO
Protect the execution of the work   130
Both from prevention and discovery.

D'AMVILLE
Here was a murder bravely carried through
The eye of observation, unobserved.

108 *induction* D'Amville's use of this technical term (meaning 'prologue') emphasizes the theatrical, contrived nature of the murder of Montferrers
116 *precisian* puritan, i.e., Languebeau Snuffe
119 *unrequested* unprompted
132–3 *carried . . . unobserved* watched, but not seen

BORACHIO
   And those that saw the passage of it made
   The instruments, yet knew not what they did.   135
D'AMVILLE
   That power of rule philosophers ascribe
   To him they call the supreme of the stars,
   Making their influences governors
   Of sublunary creatures, when their selves
   Are senseless of their operations – (*Thunder and lightning*)
                                          What!   140
   Dost start at thunder? Credit my belief,
   'Tis a mere effect of Nature,
   An exhalation hot and dry, involved
   Within a watery vapour i' the middle
   Region of the air, whose coldness   145
   Congealing that thick moisture to a cloud,
   The angry exhalation shut within
   A prison of contrary quality,
   Strives to be free, and with the violent
   Eruption through the grossness of that cloud   150
   Makes this noise we hear.
BORACHIO   'Tis a fearful noise.
D'AMVILLE
   'Tis a brave noise, and methinks graces our
   Accomplished project as a peal of ordnance
   Does a triumph; it speaks encouragement.
   Now Nature shows thee how it favoured our   155
   Performance, to forbear this noise when we
   Set forth because it should not terrify
   My brother's going home, which would have dashed

140–63 *What . . . success* as prose Q
144–5 *the middle Region of the air* the atmosphere was thought to
     have three zones, of which the highest and lowest were warm and
     the middle one cold
145 *Region* Collins (religion Q)
152 *brave* fine
154 *triumph* the formal, processional entry of a commander into a
     city after his victory

142 *a mere effect of Nature.* D'Amville's account of the cause of thunder is
     not unlike Tamburlaine's explanation that
            a fiery exhalation,
       Wrapped in the bowels of a freezing cloud,
       Fighting for passage, makes the welkin crack.
              (*I Tamburlaine*, IV.ii, 43–5)

Our purpose – to forbear this lightning
In our passage, lest it should ha' warned him   160
O' the pitfall. Then propitious Nature winked
At our proceedings; now it doth express
How that forbearance favoured our success.

BORACHIO
You have confirmed me; for it follows well
That Nature, since herself decay doth hate,   165
Should favour those that strengthen their estate.

D'AMVILLE
Our next endeavour is – since on the false
Report that Charlemont is dead depends
The fabric of the work – to credit that
With all the countenance we can.

BORACHIO   Faith, sir,   170
Even let his own inheritance, whereof
Y'have dispossessed him, countenance the act.
Spare so much out of that to give him a
Solemnity of funeral; 'twill quit
The cost and make your apprehension of   175
His death appear more confident and true.

D'AMVILLE
I'll take thy counsel. Now farewell black night,
Thou beauteous mistress of a murderer;
To honour thee, that hast accomplished all,
I'll wear thy colours at his funeral.   *Exeunt* 180

[Act II, Scene v]

Enter LEVIDULCIA *into her chamber, manned by* FRESCO

LEVIDULCIA
Th'art welcome into my chamber, Fresco. Prithee shut the
door. – Nay, thou mistakest me. Come in and shut it.

FRESCO
'Tis somewhat late, madam.

164 *confirmed* convinced
167–76 *Our . . . true* as prose Q
169 *credit* give credit to
170 *countenance* support
175 *apprehension* understanding, acceptance
s.d. *manned* escorted

LEVIDULCIA

No matter. I have somewhat to say to thee. What, is not thy
mistress towards a husband yet?   5

FRESCO

Faith, madam, she has suitors, but they will not suit her,
methinks. They will not come off lustily, it seems.

LEVIDULCIA

They will not come on lustily, thou wouldst say.

FRESCO

I mean, madam, they are not rich enough.

LEVIDULCIA

But I, Fresco, they are not bold enough. Thy mistress is of a   10
lively attractive blood, Fresco, and in troth she's o' my mind
for that. A poor spirit is poorer than a poor purse. Give me a
fellow that brings not only temptation with him, but has the
activity of wit and audacity of spirit to apply every word and
gesture of a woman's speech and behaviour to his own   15
desire, and make her believe she's the suitor herself, never
give back till he has made her yield to it.

FRESCO

Indeed among our equals, madam, but otherwise we shall be
put horribly out o'countenance.

LEVIDULCIA

Thou art deceived, Fresco. Ladies are as courteous as   20
yeomen's wives, and methinks they should be more gentle.
Hot diet and soft ease makes 'em, like wax always kept warm,
more easy to take impression. – Prithee untie my shoe. –
What, art thou shamefaced too? Go roundly to work, man.
My leg is not gouty; 'twill endure the feeling, I warrant thee.   25
Come hither, Fresco; thine ear. – 'S dainty, I mistook the
place; I missed thine ear and hit thy lip.

FRESCO

Your ladyship has made me blush.

LEVIDULCIA

That shows th'art full o'lusty blood and thou knowest not
how to use it. Let me see thy hand. Thou shouldst not be   30

---

7 *come off lustily* Fresco explains his meaning in line 9, but Levidulcia alters the preposition to make the phrase sexual

12 *A poor ... purse* Tilley S759

14–16 *to apply ... to his own desire* Levidulcia proceeds to act out
the role she has described, hoping that Fresco will take his cue
from her

26 *'S dainty* By God's dignity

shamefaced by thy hand, Fresco. Here's a brawny flesh and a
hairy skin, both signs of an able body. I do not like these
phlegmatic, smooth-skinned, soft-fleshed fellows. They are
like candied suckets when they begin to perish, which I
would always empty my closet of and give 'em my chamber-   35
maid. – I have some skill in palmistry; by this line that
stands directly against me thou shouldst be near a good fortune, Fresco, if thou hadst the grace to entertain it.

FRESCO

O what is that, madam, I pray?

LEVIDULCIA

No less than the love of a fair lady, if thou dost not lose her   40
with faint-heartedness.

FRESCO

A lady, madam? Alas, a lady is a great thing; I cannot compass her.

LEVIDULCIA

No? Why, I am a lady. Am I so great I cannot be compassed?
Clasp my waist and try.   45

FRESCO

I could find i' my heart, madam.   SEBASTIAN *knocks within*

LEVIDULCIA

'Uds body, my husband! Faint-hearted fool, I think thou
wert begotten between the North Pole and the congealed
passage. Now, like an ambitious coward that betrays himself
with fearful delay, you must suffer for the treason you never   50
committed. Go, hide thyself behind yond' arras instantly.

FRESCO *hides himself*

Enter SEBASTIAN

Sebastian! What do you here so late?

SEBASTIAN

Nothing yet, but I hope I shall.   *Kisses her*

LEVIDULCIA

Y'are very bold.

SEBASTIAN

And you very valiant, for you met me at full career.   55

---

34 *candied suckets* crystallized fruits
42 *compass* attain; but in the next line Levidulcia takes the literal
    meaning of 'encircle'
48 *congealed passage* Ribner suggests that this is the route, via the
    North Pole, to China and Japan, discovered in 1607
55 *full career* in jousting, a charge at full speed

LEVIDULCIA

You come to ha' me move your father's reconciliation.
I'll write a word or two i' your behalf.

SEBASTIAN

A word or two, madam? That you do for me will not be con-
tained in less than the compass of two sheets. But in plain
terms, shall we take the opportunity of privateness? 60

LEVIDULCIA

What to do?

SEBASTIAN

To dance the beginning of the world after the English
manner.

LEVIDULCIA

Why not after the French or Italian?

SEBASTIAN

Fie, they dance it preposterously, backward. 65

LEVIDULCIA

Are you so active to dance?

SEBASTIAN

I can shake my heels.

LEVIDULCIA

Y'are well made for't.

SEBASTIAN

Measure me from top to toe, you shall not find me differ
much from the true standard of proportion. 70

BELFOREST *knocks within*

LEVIDULCIA

I think I am accursed, Sebastian. There's one at the door
has beaten opportunity away from us. In brief, I love thee,
and it shall not be long before I give thee a testimony of it.
To save thee now from suspicion, do no more but draw thy
rapier, chafe thyself, and when he comes in rush by without 75
taking notice of him. Only seem to be angry, and let me alone
for the rest.

Enter BELFOREST

SEBASTIAN

Now by the hand of Mercury – *Exit* SEBASTIAN

BELFOREST

What's the matter, wife?

LEVIDULCIA

Ooh, ooh, husband! 80

65 *preposterously* unnaturally

BELFOREST

Prithee what ail'st thou, woman?

LEVIDULCIA

O feel my pulse. It beats, I warrant you. Be patient a little,
sweet husband; tarry but till my breath come to me again,
and I'll satisfy you.

BELFOREST

What ails Sebastian? He looks so distractedly.   85

LEVIDULCIA

The poor gentleman's almost out on's wits, I think. You
remember the displeasure his father took against him about
the liberty of speech he used even now when your daughter
went to be married?

BELFOREST

Yes, what of that?   90

LEVIDULCIA

'T has crazed him sure. He met a poor man i' the street even
now. Upon what quarrel I know not, but he pursued him so
violently that if my house had not been his rescue, he had
surely killed him.

BELFOREST

What a strange desperate young man is that!   95

LEVIDULCIA

Nay husband, he grew so in rage when he saw the man was
conveyed from him that he was ready even to have drawn his
naked weapon upon me. And had not your knocking at the
door prevented him, surely h'had done something to me.

BELFOREST

Where's the man?   100

LEVIDULCIA

Alas, here. I warrant you the poor fearful soul is scarce come
to himself again yet. [*Aside*] If the fool have any wit he will
apprehend me. [*To* FRESCO] Do you hear, sir? You may be
bold to come forth; the Fury that haunted you is gone.

              FRESCO *peeps fearfully forth from behind the arras*

FRESCO

Are you sure he is gone?   105

BELFOREST

He's gone, he's gone, I warrant thee.

FRESCO

I would I were gone too. Has shook me almost into a dead
palsy.

BELFOREST

How fell the difference between you?

FRESCO

I would I were out at the back door.   110

BELFOREST

Th'art safe enough. Prithee tell's the falling out.

FRESCO

Yes sir, when I have recovered my spirits. My memory is
almost frighted from me. – O, so, so, so. – Why, sir, as I
came along the street, sir, – this same gentleman came
stumbling after me and trod o' my heel. – I cried O. Do you   115
cry, sirrah? says he. Let me see your heel; if it be not hurt,
I'll make you cry for something. So he claps my head
between his legs and pulls off my shoe. I having shifted no
socks in a sennight, the gentleman cried Foh, and said my
feet were base and cowardly feet; they stunk for fear. Then   120
he knocked my shoe about my pate, and I cried O, once
more. In the meantime comes a shag-haired dog by and rubs
against his shins. The gentlemen took the dog in shag-hair to
be some watch-man in a rug gown, and swore he would hang
me up at the next door with my lantern in my hand, that   125
passengers might see their way as they went without
rubbing against gentleman's shins. So, for want of a cord, he
took his own garters off, and as he was going to make a noose,
I watched my time and ran away. And as I ran, indeed, I bid
him hang himself in his own garters. So he, in choler, pur-   130
sued me hither as you see.

BELFOREST

Why, this savours of distraction.

LEVIDULCIA

Of mere distraction.

FRESCO [*Aside*]

Howsoever it savours, I am sure it smells like a lie.

BELFOREST

Thou may'st go forth at the back door, honest fellow; the   135
way is private and safe.

FRESCO

So it had need, for your fore-door here is both common and
dangerous.   *Exit* BELFOREST

119 *sennight* week
130 *hang himself in his own garters* Tilley G42; the expression was a
     very common one—cf. *1 Henry IV*, 'Hang thyself in thine own
     heir-apparent garters' (II.ii, 51)
133 *mere* pure
137 *your fore-door* with his parting shot Fresco denounces Levidulcia as
     a whore whose body ('fore-door') is open to all comers ('common')

LEVIDULCIA
Good night, honest Fresco.
FRESCO
Good night, madam. If you get me kissing o' ladies again –   140
Exit FRESCO

LEVIDULCIA
This falls out handsomely.
But yet the matter does not well succeed
Till I have brought it to the very deed.   *Exit*

[Act II, Scene vi]

Enter CHARLEMONT, *in arms, a* MUSKETEER, *and a* SERGEANT

CHARLEMONT
Sergeant, what hour o' the night is 't?
SERGEANT
About one.
CHARLEMONT
I would you would relieve me, for I am
So heavy that I shall ha' much ado
To stand out my perdu.   *Thunder and lightning*
SERGEANT   I'll e'en but walk   5
The round, sir, and then presently return.
MUSKETEER
For God's sake, sergeant, relieve me. About five hours to-
gether in so foul a stormy night as this!
SERGEANT
Why 'tis a music, soldier. Heaven and earth are now in con-
sort, when the thunder and the cannon play to one another.   10
Exit SERGEANT

CHARLEMONT
I know not why I should be thus inclined
To sleep. I feel my disposition pressed
With a necessity of heaviness.
Soldier! If thou hast any better eyes,
I prithee wake me when the sergeant comes.   15
MUSKETEER
Sir, 'tis so dark and stormy that I shall

5 *perdu* the post of sentinel perdu, the most dangerous outpost duty
6 *The round* the circuit performed by the watch among the senti-
nels of a garrison
9 *in consort* in harmony (as musicians)
11–18 *I . . . wake* as prose Q

Scarce either see or hear him ere he comes
Upon me.
CHARLEMONT
    I cannot force myself to wake.   *Sleeps*

    Enter the GHOST OF MONTFERRERS

MONTFERRERS
Return to France, for thy old father's dead
And thou by murder disinherited.   20
Attend with patience the success of things,
But leave revenge unto the King of kings.   *Exit*
       CHARLEMONT *starts and wakes*
CHARLEMONT
O my affrighted soul, what fearful dream
Was this that waked me? Dreams are but the raised
Impressions of premeditated things,   25
By serious apprehension left upon
Our minds, or else th'imaginary shapes
Of objects proper to th'complexion or
The dispositions of our bodies. These
Can neither of them be the cause why I   30
Should dream thus, for my mind has not been moved
With any one conception of a thought
To such a purpose, nor my nature wont
To trouble me with fantasies of terror.
It must be something that my Genius would   35
Inform me of. Now gracious heaven forbid!
O, let my spirit be deprived of all
Foresight and knowledge ere it understand

21 *success* outcome   26 *apprehension* consideration
29 *dispositions* temperaments
35 *Genius* the attendant spirit allotted to every man at his birth—
  the Guardian Angel in Christian mythology

22 *leave revenge unto the King of kings.* This sentiment was reiterated more
  and more strongly in the seventeenth century. In *Elizabethan Revenge
  Tragedy* (1940) Fredson Bowers traces this growing disapproval of
  personal revenge.
28 *complexion.* Ribner quotes Thomas Elyot, *The Castel of Helthe*: 'Complexion is a combynation of two dyvers qualities of the foure elementes
  in one bodye, as hotte and drye of the fyre: hotte and moyste of the
  Ayre, cold and moyste of the water, colde and dry of the Erth. But
  although all these complexions be assembled in every body of man and
  woman, yet the body taketh the denomination of those qualities,
  whyche abounde in hym, more thanne in the other'.

That vision acted, or divine that act
To come. Why should I think so? Left I not   40
My worthy father i'the kind regard
Of a most loving uncle? Soldier, saw'st
No apparition of a man?
MUSKETEER   You dream,
Sir, I saw nothing.
CHARLEMONT   Tush, these idle dreams
Are fabulous. Our boiling fantasies   45
Like troubled waters falsify the shapes
Of things retained in them, and make 'em seem
Confounded when they are distinguished. So
My actions daily conversant with war,
The argument of blood and death, had left,   50
Perhaps, th'imaginary presence of
Some bloody accident upon my mind,
Which, mixed confusedly with other thoughts,
Whereof th'remembrance of my father might
Be one, presented all together seem   55
Incorporate, as if his body were
The owner of that blood, the subject of
That death, when he's at Paris and that blood
Shed here. It may be thus. I would not leave
The war, for reputation's sake, upon   60
An idle apprehension, a vain dream.

Enter the GHOST

MUSKETEER
Stand, stand, I say. No? Why then have at thee.
Sir, if you will not stand, I'll make you fall.
Nor stand, nor fall? Nay, then the Devil's dam
Has broke her husband's head, for sure it is a spirit.   65
I shot it through, and yet it will not fall.   *Exit*
The GHOST *approaches* CHARLEMONT.
He fearfully avoids it

CHARLEMONT
O pardon me. My doubtful heart was slow
To credit that which I did fear to know.

Exeunt

39 *That vision acted* that deed (which has been described in the
    dream) accomplished
41 *regard* care   45 *fabulous* false, fictional
48 *Confounded* Mixed up   56 *Incorporate* Joined into one
62–6 *Stand . . . fall* as prose Q

Act III, Scene i

Enter [D'AMVILLE *with*] *the funeral of* MONTFERRERS

D'AMVILLE

Set down the body. Pay earth what she lent,
But she shall bear a living monument
To let succeeding ages truly know
That she is satisfied what he did owe,
Both principal and use, because his worth   5
Was better at his death than at his birth.

A dead march. Enter the funeral of CHARLEMONT *as a soldier*

And with his body place that memory
Of noble Charlemont, his worthy son,
And give their graves the rites that do belong
To soldiers. They were soldiers both. The father   10
Held open war with sin, the son with blood;
This in a war more gallant, that more good.
                                                        The first volley
There place their arms, and here their epitaphs,
And may these lines survive the last of graves:

          The Epitaph of MONTFERRERS
Here lie the ashes of that earth and fire   15
  Whose heat and fruit did feed and warm the poor.
And they, as if they would in sighs expire
  And into tears dissolve, his death deplore.
He did that good freely, for goodness' sake,
  Unforced, for generousness he held so dear   20
That he feared none but Him that did him make,
  And yet he served Him more for love than fear.
    So's life provided that though he did die
    A sudden death, yet died not suddenly.

---

4 *satisfied* paid back
5 *use* interest
13 *There* on the graves, which were covered by a scaffolding on
   which mourners placed tributes
24 *suddenly* unprepared

---

2 *a living monument.* The same phrase is used, as Ribner remarks, in
Hamlet: 'This grave shall have a living monument' (V.i, 319). It is not
clear whether the monument should be a lifelike statue, or an eloquent
panegyric.

The Epitaph of CHARLEMONT
His body lies interred within this mould,   25
Who died a young man, yet departed old,
And in all strength of youth that man can have
Was ready still to drop into his grave.
For aged in virtue, with a youthful eye
He welcomed it, being still prepared to die;   30
And living so, though young deprived of breath,
He did not suffer an untimely death,
But we may say of his blest decease:
He died in war, and yet he died in peace.
                              The second volley

O might that fire revive the ashes of   35
This phoenix! Yet the wonder would not be
So great as he was good and wondered at
For that. His life's example was so true
A practique of religion's theory
That her divinity seemed rather the   40
Description than th'instruction of his life.
And of his goodness was his virtuous son
A worthy imitator. So that on
These two Herculean pillars where their arms
Are placed there may be writ *Non ultra.* For   45
Beyond their lives, as well for youth as age,
Nor young nor old, in merit or in name,
Shall e'er exceed their virtues or their fame.
                              The third volley

'Tis done. Thus fair accompliments make foul
Deeds gracious. Charlemont, come now when t'wou't,   50
I've buried under these two marble stones
Thy living hopes and thy dead father's bones.
                              Exeunt

Enter CASTABELLA *mourning, to the monument of* CHARLEMONT

CASTABELLA
    O Thou that know'st me justly Charlemont's,

28 *still* always   30 *it* i.e., death
35–6 *the ashes of This phoenix* the legendary bird destroyed itself by
    fire and rose again, re-created, from its own ashes
39 *practique* practice
44 *These two Herculean pillars* the monuments of father and son,
    compared with the pillars of Hercules set up in the Straits of
    Gibraltar forbidding seamen to pass further
45 *Non ultra* no further

Though in the forced possession of another,
Since from Thine own free spirit we receive it   55
That our affections cannot be compelled
Though our actions may, be not displeased if on
The altar of his tomb I sacrifice
My tears. They are the jewels of my love
Dissolved into grief, and fall upon   60
His blasted spring as April dew upon
A sweet young blossom shaked before the time.

Enter CHARLEMONT *with a* SERVANT

CHARLEMONT
Go see my trunks disposed of. I'll but walk
A turn or two i'th' church and follow you.   *Exit* SERVANT
O, here's the fatal monument of my   65
Dead father first presented to mine eye.
What's here? In memory of Charlemont?
Some false relation has abused belief.
I am deluded. But I thank thee, Heaven.
For ever let me be deluded thus.   70
My Castabella mourning o'er my hearse?
Sweet Castabella, rise; I am not dead.
CASTABELLA
O Heaven defend me!   *Falls in a swoon*
CHARLEMONT   I beshrew my rash
And inconsiderate passion. – Castabella! –
That could not think – my Castabella! – that   75
My sudden presence might affright her sense.
I prithee, my affection, pardon me.   *She rises*
Reduce thy understanding to thine eye.
Within this habit which thy misinformed
Conceit takes only for a shape live both   80
The soul and body of thy Charlemont.
CASTABELLA
I feel a substance warm and soft and moist,
Subject to the capacity of sense.

64 *church* i.e., churchyard
68 *relation* tale; but the modern sense 'relative' was also available,
   permitting an ironic pun
80 *Conceit* Imagination
   shape phantom
83 *capacity of sense* i.e., the qualities which Charlemont's body
   possesses (warmth, softness, and moisture) are those that can
   be physically apprehended, touched, and felt

CHARLEMONT
Which spirits are not, for their essence is
Above the nature and the order of   85
Those elements whereof our senses are
Created. Touch my lip. Why turn'st thou from me?
CASTABELLA
Grief above griefs! That which should woe relieve,
Wished and obtained, gives greater cause to grieve.
CHARLEMONT
Can Castabella think it cause of grief   90
That the relation of my death proves false?
CASTABELLA
The presence of the person we affect,
Being hopeless to enjoy him, makes our grief
More passionate than if we saw him not.
CHARLEMONT
Why not enjoy? Has absence changed thee?
CASTABELLA   Yes,   95
From maid to wife.
CHARLEMONT   Art married?
CASTABELLA   O, I am.
CHARLEMONT
Married! Had not my mother been a woman,
I should protest against the chastity
Of all thy sex. How can the merchant or
The mariner, absent whole years, from wives   100
Experienced in the satisfaction of
Desire, promise themselves to find their sheets
Unspotted with adultery at their
Return, when you that never had the sense
Of actual temptation could not stay   105
A few short months?
CASTABELLA   O, do but hear me speak.
CHARLEMONT
But thou wert wise and didst consider that
A soldier might be maimed and so perhaps
Lose his ability to please thee.
CASTABELLA   No.
That weakness pleases me in him I have.   110
CHARLEMONT
What, married to a man unable too?
O strange incontinence! Why, was thy blood

112 *incontinence* unchastity

Increased to such a pleurisy of lust
That of necessity there must a vein
Be opened, though by one that had no skill   115
To do't?

CASTABELLA
          Sir, I beseech you hear me.
CHARLEMONT   Speak.
CASTABELLA
Heaven knows I am unguilty of this act.
CHARLEMONT
Why, wert thou forced to do't?
CASTABELLA   Heaven knows I was.
CHARLEMONT
What villain did it?
CASTABELLA   Your uncle D'Amville.
And he that dispossessed my love of you   120
Hath disinherited you of possession.
CHARLEMONT
Disinherited? Wherein have I deserved
To be deprived of my dear father's love?
CASTABELLA
Both of his love and him. His soul's at rest,
But here your injured patience may behold   125
The signs of his lamented memory.
                    CHARLEMONT *finds his father's monument*
H'has found it. When I took him for a ghost
I could endure the torment of my fear
More easily than I can his sorrows hear.   *Exit*
CHARLEMONT
Of all men's griefs must mine be singular?   130
Without example? Here I met my grave,
And all men's woes are buried i' their graves
But mine. In mine my miseries are born.
I prithee, sorrow, leave a little room
In my confounded and tormented mind   135
For understanding to deliberate
The cause or author of this accident –
A close advantage of my absence made

113 *pleurisy* excess
114–15 *a vein Be opened* Charlemont's image is from blood-letting,
    the opening of a vein to drain off the supposed excess of blood
121 *possession* i.e., of your father's estate
130 *singular* unique
138 *close* secret

To dispossess me both of land and wife,
And all the profit does arise to him   140
By whom my absence was first moved and urged.
These circumstances, uncle, tell me you
Are the suspected author of those wrongs,
Whereof the lightest is more heavy than
The strongest patience can endure to bear.   *Exit* 145

[Act III, Scene ii]

Enter D'AMVILLE, SEBASTIAN, *and* LANGUEBEAU [SNUFFE]

D'AMVILLE
  Now sir, your business?
SEBASTIAN   My annuity.
D'AMVILLE
  Not a denier.
SEBASTIAN   How would you ha' me live?
D'AMVILLE
  Why, turn crier. Cannot you turn crier?
SEBASTIAN
  Yes.
D'AMVILLE
      Then do so; y'have a good voice for't.
  Y'are excellent at crying of a rape.   5
SEBASTIAN
  Sir, I confess in particular respect to yourself I was some-
  what forgetful. General honesty possessed me.
D'AMVILLE
  Go, th'art the base corruption of my blood,
  And like a tetter grow'st unto my flesh.
SEBASTIAN
  Inflict any punishment upon me. The severity shall not   10
  discourage me if it be not shameful, so you'll but put money
  i' my purse. The want of money makes a free spirit more mad
  than the possession does an usurer.
D'AMVILLE
  Not a farthing.

---

2 *denier* a coin of little value
3 *crier* town crier
9 *tetter* a skin-disease such as eczema
11–12 *but put money i' my purse* The words are those of Iago to Rod-
    erigo: 'Put money in thy purse' (*Othello*, I.iii, 340)

SEBASTIAN

    Would you ha' me turn purse-taker? 'Tis the next way to   15
    do't. For want is like the rack; it draws a man to endanger
    himself to the gallows rather than endure it.

Enter CHARLEMONT; D'AMVILLE *counterfeits to take him for a*
ghost

D'AMVILLE

    What art thou? Stay! Assist my troubled sense.
    My apprehension will distract me. Stay!

          LANGUEBEAU SNUFFE *avoids him fearfully*

SEBASTIAN

    What art thou? Speak!

CHARLEMONT   The spirit of Charlemont.   20

D'AMVILLE

    O stay. Compose me. I dissolve.

LANGUEBEAU

    No, 'tis profane. Spirits are invisible. 'Tis the fiend i' th'
    likeness of Charlemont. I will have no conversation with
    Satan.

                    Exit [LANGUEBEAU] SNUFFE

SEBASTIAN

    The spirit of Charlemont? I'll try that.   25
              Strike[s], and the blow [is] returned
    'Fore God, thou sayest true; th'art all spirit.

D'AMVILLE

    Go call the officers.

                       Exit D'AMVILLE

CHARLEMONT

    Th'art a villain and the son of a villain.

SEBASTIAN

    You lie.

             [They] fight. SEBASTIAN *is down*

CHARLEMONT

    Have at thee.   30

        Enter the GHOST OF MONTFERRERS

    Revenge, to thee I'll dedicate this work.

MONTFERRERS

    Hold, Charlemont!
    Let Him revenge my murder and thy wrongs
    To whom the justice of revenge belongs.   *Exit*

15 *purse-taker* pickpocket   33 *Let Him revenge* cf. II.vi, 22 and *note*

CHARLEMONT
　You torture me between the passion of   35
　My blood and the religion of my soul.

                                        SEBASTIAN *rises*

SEBASTIAN
　A good honest fellow.

　　　Enter D'AMVILLE [*and* BORACHIO] *with* OFFICERS

D'AMVILLE
　What, wounded? Apprehend him. Sir, is this
　Your salutation for the courtesy
　I did you when we parted last? You ha'   40
　Forgot I lent you a thousand crowns. [*To the* OFFICERS] First
　　　　　　　　　　　　　　　　　　　　　　　let
　Him answer for this riot. When the law
　Is satisfied for that, an action for
　His debt shall clap him up again. [*To* CHARLEMONT] I took
　You for a spirit, and I'll conjure you   45
　Before I ha' done.
CHARLEMONT   No, I'll turn conjurer. Devil!
　Within this circle, in the midst of all
　Thy force and malice, I conjure thee do
　Thy worst.
D'AMVILLE   Away with him.
　　　　　　　　　　Exeunt OFFICERS *with* CHARLEMONT
SEBASTIAN   Sir, I have got
　A scratch or two here for your sake. I hope   50
　You'll give me money to pay the surgeon.
D'AMVILLE
　Borachio, fetch me a thousand crowns. [*Exit* BORACHIO] I am
　Content to countenance the freedom of
　Your spirit when 'tis worthily employed.
　A' God's name, give behaviour the full scope   55
　Of gen'rous liberty, but let it not
　Disperse and spend itself in courses of
　Unbounded licence. [BORACHIO *returns with money*] Here,
　　　　　　　　　　　　　　　　　　pay for your hurts.
　　　　　　　　　　　　　　　　　　Exit D'AMVILLE

SEBASTIAN
　I thank you, sir. 'Gen'rous liberty' – that is to say, freely to

35–6　*You . . . soul* as prose Q
38–58　*What . . . hurts* as prose Q
47　*this circle* the magician's circle was an essential adjunct for con-
　　juring; cf. *Dr Faustus*, I.iii

bestow my abilities to honest purposes. Methinks I 60
should not follow that instruction now, if having the means to
do an honest office for an honest fellow, I should neglect it.
Charlemont lies in prison for a thousand crowns, and here I
have a thousand crowns. Honesty tells me 'twere well done to
release Charlemont. But discretion says I had much ado to 65
come by this, and when this shall be gone I know not where
to finger any more, especially if I employ it to this use, which
is like to endanger me into my father's perpetual displeasure.
And then I may go hang myself, or be forced to do that will
make another save me the labour. No matter. Charlemont, 70
thou gavest me my life, and that's somewhat of a purer earth
than gold, as fine as it is. 'Tis no courtesy I do thee, but
thankfulness. I owe thee it and I'll pay it. He fought bravely,
but the officers dragged him villainously. Arrant knaves!
For using him so discourteously, may the sins o' the poor 75
people be so few that you sha' not be able to spare so much
out o' your gettings as will pay for the hire of a lame starved
hackney to ride to an execution, but go a-foot to the gallows
and be hanged. May elder brothers turn good husbands and
younger brothers get good wives, that there be no need of 80
debt-books nor use of sergeants. May there be all peace but i'
the war and all charity but i' the devil, so that prisons may be
turned to hospitals, though the officers live o' the benevo-
lence. If this curse might come to pass, the world would
say, *Blessed be he that curseth.* 85

Exit

[Act III, Scene iii]

Enter CHARLEMONT *in prison*

CHARLEMONT

I grant thee, Heaven, thy goodness doth command
Our punishments, but yet no further than
The measure of our sins. How should they else
Be just? Or how should that good purpose of
Thy justice take effect by bounding men   5
Within the confines of humanity,
When our afflictions do exceed our crimes?
Then they do rather teach the barb'rous world
Examples that extend her cruelties
Beyond their own dimensions, and instruct   10

3 *they* i.e., punishments

Our actions to be more, more barbarous.
O my afflicted soul, how torment swells
Thy apprehension with profane conceit
Against the sacred justice of my God!
Our own constructions are the authors of   15
Our misery. We never measure our
Conditions but with men above us in
Estate, so while our spirits labour to
Be higher than our fortunes, th'are more base.
Since all those attributes which make men seem   20
Superior to us are man's subjects and
Were made to serve him, the repining man
Is of a servile spirit to deject
The value of himself below their estimation.

Enter SEBASTIAN *with the* KEEPER

SEBASTIAN

Here, take my sword. – How now, my wild swaggerer, y'are   25
tame enough now, are you not? The penury of a prison is
like a soft consumption. 'Twill humble the pride o' your
mortality and arm your soul in complete patience to endure
the weight of affliction without feeling it. What, hast no
music in thee? Th' hast trebles and basses enough, treble   30
injury and base usage. But trebles and basses make poor
music without means. Thou wantest means, dost? What,
dost droop? Art dejected?

CHARLEMONT

No, sir. I have a heart above the reach
Of thy most violent maliciousness,   35
A fortitude in scorn of thy contempt –
Since Fate is pleased to have me suffer it –
That can bear more than thou hast power t'inflict.
I was a baron; that thy father has
Deprived me of. Instead of that I am   40
Created king. I've lost a signory
That was confined within a piece of earth,
A wart upon the body of the world.
But now I am an emp'ror of a world,
This little world of man. My passions are   45

32 *means* in music, the middle part between the bass and the treble
41 *signory* estate
45 *This little world of man* Charlemont's phrase encapsulates the
Renaissance teaching that the body of man, the microcosm, was
an exact replica of the earth, the macrocosm

My subjects, and I can command them laugh,
Whilst thou dost tickle 'em to death with misery.

SEBASTIAN

'Tis bravely spoken, and I love thee for 't. Thou liest here
for a thousand crowns. Here are a thousand to redeem thee –
not for the ransom o' my life thou gavest me; that I value   50
not at one crown. 'Tis none o' my deed; thank my father
for 't. 'Tis his goodness. Yet he looks not for thanks, for he
does it underhand, out of a reserved disposition to do thee
good without ostentation. – Out o' great heart you'll
refuse't now, will you?   55

CHARLEMONT

No. Since I must submit myself to Fate,
I never will neglect the offer of
One benefit, but entertain them as
Her favours and th'inductions to some end
Of better fortune, as whose instrument   60
I thank thy courtesy.

SEBASTIAN   Well, come along.   *Exeunt*

[Act III, Scene iv]

Enter D'AMVILLE *and* CASTABELLA

D'AMVILLE

Daughter, you do not well to urge me. I
Ha' done no more than justice. Charlemont
Shall die and rot in prison, and 'tis just.

CASTABELLA

O father, mercy is an attribute
As high as justice, an essential part   5
Of His unbounded goodness, whose divine
Impression, form, and image man should bear.
And methinks man should love to imitate
His mercy, since the only countenance
Of justice were destruction, if the sweet   10
And loving favour of His mercy did
Not mediate between it and our weakness.

D'AMVILLE

Forbear. You will displease me. He shall rot.

56–61 *No . . . along* as prose Q

4ff. Castabella's speech demands comparison with the great 'mercy'
speeches in *Measure for Measure* (II.ii, 59–79) and *The Merchant of
Venice* (IV.i, 180–93).

CASTABELLA
    Dear sir, since by your greatness you
    Are nearer Heaven in place, be nearer it   15
    In goodness. Rich men should transcend the poor
    As clouds the earth, raised by the comfort of
    The sun to water dry and barren grounds.
    If neither the impression in your soul
    Of goodness, nor the duty of your place   20
    As Goodness' substitute can move you, then
    Let Nature, which in savages, in beasts,
    Can stir to pity, tell you that he is
    Your kinsman.
D'AMVILLE   You expose your honesty
    To strange construction. Why should you so urge
    Release for Charlemont? Come, you profess
    More nearness to him than your modesty
    Can answer. You have tempted my suspicion.
    I tell thee he shall starve, and die, and rot.

Enter CHARLEMONT *and* SEBASTIAN

CHARLEMONT
    Uncle, I thank you.
D'AMVILLE   Much good do it you.   30
    Who did release him?
SEBASTIAN   I.

                                Exit CASTABELLA
D'AMVILLE   You are a villain.
SEBASTIAN
    Y'are my father.   *Exit* SEBASTIAN
D'AMVILLE [*Aside*] I must temporize.
    [*To* CHARLEMONT] Nephew, had not his open freedom made
    My disposition known, I would ha' borne
    The course and inclination of my love   35
    According to the motion of the sun,
    Invisibly enjoyed and understood.
CHARLEMONT
    That shows your good works are directed to

20–1 *your place As Goodness' substitute* as magistrate, the representa-
    tive of Divine Justice
36 *According to* Like

---

14 *your greatness.* The example the great should be to the humble forms
    part of the Cardinal's sermon to the Duke in Middleton's *Women*
    Beware Women, IV.i, 199–226.

No other end than goodness. I was rash,
I must confess, but –
D'AMVILLE   I will excuse you.   40
To lose a father and, as you may think,
Be disinherited, it must be granted,
Are motives to impatience. But for death,
Who can avoid it? And for his estate,
In the uncertainty of both your lives   45
'Twas done discreetly to confer't upon
A known successor, being the next in blood,
And one, dear nephew, whom in time to come
You shall have cause to thank. I will not be
Your dispossessor, but your guardian.   50
I will supply your father's vacant place,
To guide your green improvidence of youth
And make you ripe for your inheritance.
CHARLEMONT
Sir, I embrace your generous promises.   [*They embrace*]

Enter ROUSARD *sick, and* CASTABELLA

ROUSARD
Embracing? I behold the object that   55
Mine eye affects. Dear cousin Charlemont!
D'AMVILLE
My elder son. He meets you happily,
For with the hand of our whole family
We interchange th'indenture of our loves.
CHARLEMONT
And I accept it, yet not joyfully   60
Because y'are sick.
D'AMVILLE   Sir, his affection's sound
Though he be sick in body.
ROUSARD   Sick indeed.
A general weakness did surprise my health
The very day I married Castabella.
As if my sickness were a punishment   65
That did arrest me for some injury
I then committed. [*To* CASTABELLA] Credit me, my love,
I pity thy ill fortune to be matched
With such a weak unpleasing bedfellow.
CASTABELLA
Believe me, sir, it never troubles me.   70

59 *indenture* formal declaration

I am as much respectless to enjoy
Such pleasure as ignorant what it is.

CHARLEMONT

Thy sex's wonder. Unhappy Charlemont.

D'AMVILLE

Come, let's to supper. There we will confirm
The eternal bond of our concluded love.   *Exeunt*   75

Act IV, Scene i

Enter CATAPLASMA *and* SOQUETTE *with needlework*

CATAPLASMA

Come, Soquette, your work; let's examine your work.
What's here? A medlar with a plum tree growing hard by
it, the leaves o' the plum tree falling off, the gum issuing
out o' the perished joints, and the branches some of 'em
dead and some rotten, and yet but a young plum tree. In   5
good sooth, very pretty.

SOQUETTE

The plum tree, forsooth, grows so near the medlar that the
medlar sucks and draws all the sap from it and the natural
strength o' the ground, so that it cannot prosper.

CATAPLASMA

How conceited you are! But here th'hast made a tree to   10
bear no fruit. Why's that?

SOQUETTE

There grows a savin tree next it, forsooth.

---

71 *respectless* indifferent

Almost every word glossed in this scene is susceptible of a second,
obscene, interpretation; but to point out every bawdy joke would
destroy the wit. Comment has therefore been reserved for necessary
elucidation.

  2 *medlar* a kind of pear-tree whose fruit bears some resemblance to
    the female genitals and which was often used with this meaning
    in the sixteenth and seventeenth centuries; cf. *Romeo and Juliet*,
    II.i, 35–6:
        And wish his mistress were that kind of fruit
        As maids call medlars, when they laugh alone
  2 *plum tree* 'then Hey ding a ding, up with your petticoats, have at
    your plum-tree' (Nashe, *Have With You to Saffron-Walden*,
    Works, ed. McKerrow, III, 113)
 10 *conceited* witty
 12 *savin tree* the poisonous tops and berries of the savin tree (a small
    evergreen) were widely used as abortifacients

CATAPLASMA
Forsooth, you are a little too witty in that.

Enter SEBASTIAN

SEBASTIAN [*Embracing her*]
But this honeysuckle winds about this whitethorn very
prettily and lovingly, sweet Mistress Cataplasma.   15
CATAPLASMA
Monsieur Sebastian! In good sooth, very uprightly welcome
this evening.
SEBASTIAN
What, moralizing upon this gentlewoman's needlework?
Let's see.
CATAPLASMA
No, sir, only examining whether it be done to the true   20
nature and life o' the thing.
SEBASTIAN
Here y' have set a medlar with a bachelor's button o' one
side and a snail o' th' t'other. The bachelor's button
should have held his head up more pertly towards the medlar;
the snail o' th' t'other side should ha' been wrought with   25
an artificial laziness, doubling his tail and putting out his
horn but half the length, and then the medlar falling, as it
were, from the lazy snail and inclining towards the pert
bachelor's button, their branches spreading and winding
one within another as if they did embrace. But here's a   30
moral. A poppring pear tree growing upon the bank of a
river, seeming continually to look downwards into the
water as if it were enamoured of it, and ever as the fruit
ripens lets it fall for love, as it were, into her lap; which
the wanton stream, like a strumpet, no sooner receives   35
but she carries it away and bestows it upon some other
creature she maintains, still seeming to play and dally
under the poppring so long that it has almost washed away
the earth from the root, and now the poor tree stands as if
it were ready to fall and perish by that whereon it spent all   40
the substance it had.

22 *bachelor's button* the double variety of the common buttercup (but
   also any double variety of a wild flower), worn by lovers
23 *snail* 'a traditional symbol of sexual potency' (Ribner)
31 *poppring pear tree* this is the opposite of the medlar; its fruit is
   shaped like the male sexual organ; cf. *Romeo and Juliet*, II.i, 37–8:
         O Romeo! that she were, O! that she were
         An open et caetera, thou a poperin pear

CATAPLASMA

Moral for you that love those wanton running waters.

SEBASTIAN

But is not my Lady Levidulcia come yet?

CATAPLASMA

Her purpose promised us her company ere this. *Lirie*, your
lute and your book.   45

SEBASTIAN

Well said. A lesson o' th' lute to entertain the time with till
she comes.

CATAPLASMA

Sol, fa, mi, la – Mi, mi, mi – 'Precious! Dost not see *mi*
between the two crotchets? Strike me full there. So –
forward. – This is a sweet strain, and thou fingerest it   50
beastly. *Mi* is a large there, and the prick that stands
before *mi* a long; always halve your note. Now – run your
division pleasingly with those quavers. Observe all your
graces i' th' touch. Here's a sweet close – strike it full; it sets
off your music delicately.   55

Enter LANGUEBEAU SNUFFE *and* LEVIDULCIA

LANGUEBEAU

Purity be in this house.

CATAPLASMA

'Tis now entered, and welcome with your good ladyship.

SEBASTIAN

Cease that music. Here's a sweeter instrument.

                                        [*Goes to embrace her*]

LEVIDULCIA

Restrain your liberty. See you not Snuffe?

SEBASTIAN

What does the stinkard here? Put Snuffe out. He's offensive.   60

LEVIDULCIA

No. The credit of his company defends my being abroad
from the eye of suspicion.

---

44 *Lirie* there seems to be no explanation for this; maybe it is just a
   variant of 'tra la la'
48 *'Precious* ed. (Precious Q) By God's precious blood
51 *large* 'a maxim, one kind of single note in the system of "men-
   sural notation" developed by Franco of Cologne around 1250
   and in use until about 1600' (Ribner)
53 *division* 'the execution of a rapid melodic passage, conceived as
   the division of a series of long notes into shorter ones' (Ribner)
54 *close* finale

CATAPLASMA

Will 't please your ladyship go up into the closet?
There are those falls and tires I told you of.

LEVIDULCIA

Monsieur Snuffe, I shall request your patience. My stay will   65
not be long.

Exit with SEBASTIAN

LANGUEBEAU

My duty, madam. Falls and tires? I begin to suspect
what falls and tires you mean. My lady and Sebastian the fall
and the tire, and I the shadow. I perceive the purity of my
conversation is used but for a property to cover the un-   70
cleanness of their purposes. The very contemplation o'
th' thing makes the spirit of the flesh begin to wriggle in
my blood. And here my desire has met with an object
already. This gentlewoman, methinks, should be swayed
with the motion, living in a house where moving example is   75
so common. Temptation has prevailed over me, and I will
attempt to make it overcome her. – Mistress Cataplasma,
my lady, it seems, has some business that requires her stay.
The fairness o' th' evening invites me into the air; will it
please you give this gentlewoman leave to leave her work   80
and walk a turn or two with me for honest recreation?

CATAPLASMA

With all my heart, sir. Go, Soquette, give ear to his instructions. You may get understanding by his company, I
can tell you.

LANGUEBEAU

In the way of holiness, Mistress Cataplasma.   85

CATAPLASMA

Good Monsieur Snuffe! I will attend your return.

LANGUEBEAU [*To* SOQUETTE]

Your hand, gentlewoman.
[*Aside*] The flesh is humble till the spirit move it,
But when 'tis raised it will command above it.

Exeunt

64 *falls and tires* veils and hats
69 *shadow* a border attached to the bonnet which protected a lady's
complexion

[Act IV, Scene ii]

Enter D'AMVILLE, CHARLEMONT, *and* BORACHIO

D'AMVILLE
Your sadness and the sickness of my son
Have made our company and conference
Less free and pleasing than I purposed it.
CHARLEMONT
Sir, for the present I am much unfit
For conversation or society.   5
With pardon I will rudely take my leave.
D'AMVILLE
Good night, dear nephew.   *Exit* CHARLEMONT
                    Seest thou that same man?
BORACHIO
Your meaning, sir?
D'AMVILLE   That fellow's life, Borachio,
Like a superfluous letter in the law,
Endangers our assurance.
BORACHIO   Scrape him out.   10
D'AMVILLE
Wou't do 't?
BORACHIO   Give me your purpose; I will do't.
D'AMVILLE
Sad melancholy has drawn Charlemont,
With meditation on his father's death,
Into the solitary walk behind the church.
BORACHIO
The churchyard? This the fittest place for death.   15
Perhaps he's praying. Then he's fit to die.
We'll send him charitably to his grave.
D'AMVILLE
No matter how thou tak'st him. First take this.
                    [*Gives him a*] *pistol*
Thou know'st the place. Observe his passages,
And with the most advantage make a stand,   20
That favoured by the darkness of the night,

9 *a superfluous letter in the law* a single letter (or mark of punctuation) in a legal document might seriously alter the meaning—
  hence the precision of legal jargon
10 *Scrape* it is not enough simply to cross out a 'superfluous letter',
  it must be completely erased
11 *Give me your purpose* tell me your intention

His breast may fall upon thee at so near
A distance that he sha' not shun the blow.
The deed once done, thou may'st retire with safety.
The place is unfrequented, and his death   25
Will be imputed to th'attempt of thieves.

BORACHIO

Be careless. Let your mind be free and clear.
This pistol shall discharge you of your fear.   *Exit*

D'AMVILLE

But let me call my projects to account,
For what effect and end I have engaged   30
Myself in all this blood. To leave a state
To the succession of my proper blood.
But how shall that succession be continued?
Not in my elder son, I fear. Disease
And weakness have disabled him for issue.   35
For th' t'other, his loose humour will endure
No bond of marriage. And I doubt his life;
His spirit is so boldly dangerous.
O pity that the profitable end
Of such a prosp'rous murder should be lost!   40
Nature forbid. I hope I have a body
That will not suffer me to lose my labour
For want of issue yet. But then 't must be
A bastard. Tush, they only father bastards
That father other men's begettings. Daughter!   45
Be it mine own, let it come whence it will.
I am resolved. Daughter!

Enter SERVANT

SERVANT   My lord.

D'AMVILLE

I prithee call my daughter.

Enter CASTABELLA

CASTABELLA

Your pleasure, sir?
D'AMVILLE   Is thy husband i' bed?
CASTABELLA

Yes, my lord.

27 *careless* carefree
37 *doubt* fear for

D'AMVILLE   The evening's fair. I prithee   50
Walk a turn or two.
CASTABELLA   Come, Jaspar.
D'AMVILLE   No.
We'll walk but to the corner o' the church
And I have something to speak privately.
CASTABELLA
No matter; stay.   *Exit* SERVANT
D'AMVILLE   This falls out happily.   *Exeunt*

[Act IV, Scene iii]

Enter CHARLEMONT, BORACHIO *dogging him in the churchyard.*
The clock strikes twelve

CHARLEMONT
Twelve.
BORACHIO
'Tis a good hour; 'twill strike one anon.
CHARLEMONT
How fit a place for contemplation
Is this dead of night, among the dwellings
Of the dead. This grave – perhaps th'inhabitant   5
Was in his lifetime the possessor of
His own desires. Yet in the midst of all
His greatness and his wealth, he was less rich
And less contented than in this poor piece
Of earth, lower and lesser than a cottage,   10
For here he neither wants nor cares. Now that
His body savours of corruption,
He enjoys a sweeter rest than e'er he did
Amongst the sweetest pleasures of this life,
For here there's nothing troubles him. – And there –   15
In that grave lies another. He, perhaps,
Was in his life as full of misery
As this of happiness; and here's an end
Of both. Now both their states are equal. O,
That man with so much labour should aspire   20
To worldly height, when in the humble earth
The world's condition's at the best! Or scorn
Inferior men, since to be lower than
A worm is to be higher than a king.

1–36 *Twelve . . . end* as prose Q

BORACHIO
  Then fall and rise.
                    Discharges [the pistol, which] gives false fire
CHARLEMONT   What villain's hand was that?   25
  Save thee or thou shalt perish.   *They fight*
BORACHIO   Zounds, unsaved, I think.
                                              Fall[s]

CHARLEMONT
  What, have I killed him? Whatsoe'er thou beest,
  I would thy hand had prospered, for I was
  Unfit to live and well prepared to die.
  What shall I do? Accuse myself, submit   30
  Me to the law, and that will quickly end
  This violent increase of misery?
  But 'tis a murder to be accessory
  To mine own death. I will not. I will take
  This opportunity to 'scape. It may   35
  Be Heaven reserves me to some better end.
                              Exit CHARLEMONT

Enter [LANGUEBEAU] SNUFFE *and* SOQUETTE *into the churchyard*

SOQUETTE
  Nay, good sir, I dare not. In good sooth I come of a genera-
  tion both by father and mother that were all as fruitful as
  costermongers' wives.
LANGUEBEAU
  Tush, then a tympany is the greatest danger can be feared.   40
  Their fruitfulness turns but to a certain kind of phlegmatic
  windy disease.
SOQUETTE
  I must put my understanding to your trust, sir. I would
  be loath to be deceived.
LANGUEBEAU
  No, conceive thou sha't not. Yet thou shalt profit by my   45
  instruction too. My body is not every day drawn dry,
  wench.
SOQUETTE
  Yet methinks, sir, your want of use should rather make your
  body like a well: the lesser 'tis drawn, the sooner it grows
  dry.   50

25 s.d. *gives false fire* misfires
26 *Save thee* Escape
40 *tympany* abdominal distension
49 *like a well* proverbial—Tilley W262

5—TAT • •

LANGUEBEAU
Thou shalt try that instantly.

SOQUETTE
But we want place and opportunity.

LANGUEBEAU
We have both. This is the back side of the house which the
superstitious call Saint Winifred's church, and is verily a
convenient unfrequented place,   55
Where under the close curtains of the night –

SOQUETTE
You purpose i' th' dark to make me light.
                    [SNUFFE] *pulls out a sheet, a hair, and a beard*
But what ha' you there?

LANGUEBEAU
This disguise is for security sake, wench. There's a talk,
thou know'st, that the ghost of old Montferrers walks. In   60
this church he was buried. Now if any stranger fall upon us
before our business be ended, in this disguise I shall be
taken for that ghost and never be called to examination, I
warrant thee. Thus we shall 'scape both prevention and
discovery. How do I look in this habit, wench?   65

SOQUETTE
So like a ghost that, notwithstanding I have some fore-
knowledge of you, you make my hair stand almost on end.

LANGUEBEAU
I will try how I can kiss in this beard. – O, fie, fie, fie.
I will put it off, and then kiss, and then put it on. I can do the
rest without kissing.   70

Enter CHARLEMONT *doubtfully, with his sword drawn.* [*He*] *is
upon them before they are aware. They run out divers ways
and leave the disguise*

CHARLEMONT
What ha' we here? A sheet, a hair, a beard?
What end was this disguise intended for?
No matter what. I'll not expostulate
The purpose of a friendly accident.
Perhaps it may accommodate my 'scape.   75
I fear I am pursued. For more assurance,
I'll hide me here i' th' charnel house,
This convocation-house of dead men's skulls.

57 s.d. *a hair* a wig
71–206 *What . . . best* as prose Q
73 *expostulate* question   78 s.d. *a death's head* a skull

To get into the charnel house he takes hold of a death's head; it
slips and staggers him

Death's head, deceiv'st my hold?
Such is the trust to all mortality.   80

Hides himself in the charnel house

Enter D'AMVILLE *and* CASTABELLA

CASTABELLA
My lord, the night grows late. Your lordship spake
Of something you desired to move in private.
D'AMVILLE
Yes, now I'll speak it. Th'argument is love.
The smallest ornament of thy sweet form,
That abstract of all pleasure, can command   85
The senses into passion, and thy entire
Perfection is my object; yet I love
Thee with the freedom of my reason. I
Can give thee reason for my love.
CASTABELLA   Love me,
My lord? I do believe it, for I am   90
The wife of him you love.
D'AMVILLE   'Tis true. By my
Persuasion thou wert forced to marry one
Unable to perform the office of
A husband. I was author of the wrong.
My conscience suffers under't, and I would   95
Disburden it by satisfaction.
CASTABELLA   How?
D'AMVILLE
I will supply that pleasure to thee which
He cannot.
CASTABELLA   Are y' a devil or a man?
D'AMVILLE
A man, and such a man as can return
Thy entertainment with as prodigal   100
A body as the covetous desire
Of woman ever was delighted with;
So that, besides the full performance of
Thy empty husband's duty, thou shalt have
The joy of children to continue the   105
Succession of thy blood; for the appetite
That steals her pleasure, draws the forces of
The body to an united strength and puts
'Em altogether into action,

Never fails of procreation.   110
All the purposes of man
Aim but at one of these two ends, pleasure
Or profit, and in this one sweet conjunction
Of our loves they both will meet. Would it
Not grieve thee that a stranger to thy blood   115
Should lay the first foundation of his house
Upon the ruins of thy family?

CASTABELLA
Now Heav'n defend me! May my memory
Be utterly extinguished, and the heir
Of him that was my father's enemy   120
Raise his eternal monument upon
Our ruins, ere the greatest pleasure or
The greatest profit ever tempt me to
Continue it by incest.

D'AMVILLE   Incest? Tush!
These distances affinity observes   125
Are articles of bondage cast upon
Our freedoms by our own subjections.
Nature allows a general liberty
Of generation to all creatures else.
Shall man, to whose command and use all creatures   130
Were made subject, be less free than they?

CASTABELLA
O God,
Is Thy unlimited and infinite

---

125 *affinity* kinship
127 *subjections* submissions

---

125 ff. The source of this passage, as of almost every other rationalizing of
incest in the drama of this period, is, as Collins pointed out, Ovid's
Metamorphoses Book X (lines 359 ff. in Golding's translation):
 For every other living wyght dame nature dooth permit
 To match without offence of sin. The Heifer thinkes no shame
 To beare her father on her backe: The horse bestrydes the same
 Of whom he is the syre: the Gote dooth bucke the kid that hee
 Himself begate . . .
Malefort in Massinger's *Unnatural Combat* utters the same sentiments:
 Universal nature,
 As every day 'tis evident, allows it
 To creatures of all kinds: the gallant horse
 Covers the mare to which he was the sire . . .
            (V.ii)

Omnipotence less free because Thou dost
No ill? Or if you argue merely out   135
Of Nature, do you not degenerate
From that, and are you not unworthy the
Prerogative of Nature's masterpiece,
When basely you prescribe yourself
Authority and law from their examples   140
Whom you should command? I could confute
You, but the horror of the argument
Confounds my understanding. – Sir, I know
You do but try me in your son's behalf,
Suspecting that my strength and youth of blood   145
Cannot contain themselves with impotence.
Believe me, sir,
I never wronged him. If it be your lust,
O quench it on their prostituted flesh,
Whose trade of sin can please desire with more   150
Delight and less offence. – The poison of
Your breath, evaporated from so foul a soul,
Infects the air more than the damps that rise
From bodies but half rotten in their graves.

D'AMVILLE

Kiss me. I warrant thee my breath is sweet.   155
These dead men's bones lie here of purpose to
Invite us to supply the number of
The living. Come, we'll get young bones and do't.
I will enjoy thee. No? Nay then invoke
Your great supposed protector. I will do't.   160

CASTABELLA

Supposed protector? Are y' an atheist? Then
I know my prayers and tears are spent in vain.
O patient Heav'n, why dost thou not express
Thy wrath in thunderbolts, to tear the frame
Of man in pieces? How can earth endure   165
The burden of this wickedness without
An earthquake, or the angry face of Heaven
Be not enflamed with lightning?

D'AMVILLE   Conjure up
The devil and his dam; cry to the graves;
The dead can hear thee invocate their help.   170

146 *contain* content
153 *damps* gases

CASTABELLA
　O would this grave might open, and my body
　Were bound to the dead carcass of a man
　For ever, ere it entertain the lust
　Of this detested villain.
D'AMVILLE　　　　　　　Tereus-like,
　Thus I will force my passage to –
CHARLEMONT　　　　　　　The devil!　　　　　175
　CHARLEMONT *rises in the disguise and frights* D'AMVILLE *away*
　Now lady, with the hand of Charlemont
　I thus redeem you from the arm of lust.
　My Castabella!
CASTABELLA　　My dear Charlemont!
CHARLEMONT
　For all my wrongs I thank thee, gracious Heaven;
　Th'hast made me satisfaction, to reserve　　　180
　Me for this blessed purpose. Now, sweet death,
　I'll bid thee welcome. Come, I'll guard thee home,
　And then I'll cast myself into the arms
　Of apprehension, that the law may make
　This worthy work the crown of all my actions,　185
　Being the best and last.
CASTABELLA　　　　　The last? The law?
　Now Heaven forbid, what ha' you done?
CHARLEMONT　　　　　　　Why, I have killed
　A man, not murdered him, my Castabella;
　He would ha' murdered me.
CASTABELLA　　　　　Then, Charlemont,
　The hand of Heaven directed thy defence.　　　190
　That wicked atheist, I suspect his plot.
CHARLEMONT
　My life he seeks. I would he had it, since
　He has deprived me of those blessings that
　Should make me love it. Come, I'll give it him.
CASTABELLA
　You sha' not. I will first expose myself　　　195
　To certain danger than for my defence
　Destroy the man that saved me from destruction.
CHARLEMONT
　Thou canst not satisfy me better than

174 *Tereus* Tereus king of Thrace raped his sister-in-law Philomela,
　cut out her tongue, and locked her in a secluded tower so that she
　could not betray him

To be the instrument of my release
From misery.
CASTABELLA   Then work it by escape.   200
   Leave me to this protection that still guards
   The innocent, or I will be a partner
   In your destiny.
CHARLEMONT
   My soul is heavy. Come, lie down to rest;
   These are the pillows whereon men sleep best.   205
                They lie down with either of them a death's head for a
                                                          pillow

                Enter [LANGUEBEAU] SNUFFE *seeking* SOQUETTE

LANGUEBEAU
   Soquette, Soquette, Soquette! O art thou there?
                He mistakes the body of BORACHIO *for* SOQUETTE
   Verily thou liest in a fine premeditate readiness for the
   purpose. Come, kiss me, sweet Soquette. – Now purity
   defend me from the sin of Sodom! This is a creature of
   the masculine gender. – Verily the man is blasted. – Yea,   210
   cold and stiff! – Murder, murder, murder.
                                                          Exit

Enter D'AMVILLE *distractedly;* [*he*] *starts at the sight of a*
                     death's head

D'AMVILLE
   Why dost thou stare upon me? Thou art not
   The skull of him I murdered. What hast thou
   To do to vex my conscience? Sure thou wert
   The head of a most dogged usurer,   215
   Th'art so uncharitable. And that bawd,
   The sky there, she could shut the windows and
   The doors of this great chamber of the world,
   And draw the curtains of the clouds between
   Those lights and me about this bed of earth,   220
   When that same strumpet, Murder, and myself
   Committed sin together. Then she could
   Leave us i' th' dark till the close deed
   Was done, but now that I begin to feel
   The loathsome horror of my sin and, like   225
   A lecher emptied of his lust, desire
   To bury my face under my eyebrows and

212–64 *Why . . . Committed* as prose Q

Would steal from my shame unseen, she meets me
I' th' face with all her light corrupted eyes
To challenge payment o' me. O behold!   230
Yonder's the ghost of old Montferrers in
A long white sheet, climbing yond' lofty mountain
To complain to Heav'n of me. Montferrers!
'Pox o' fearfulness. 'Tis nothing but
A fair white cloud. Why, was I born a coward?   235
He lies that says so. Yet the countenance of
A bloodless worm might ha' the courage now
To turn my blood to water. The trembling motion
Of an aspen leaf would make me, like
The shadow of that leaf, lie shaking under 't.   240
I could now commit a murder, were
It but to drink the fresh warm blood of him
I murdered, to supply the want and weakness
O' mine own, 'tis grown so cold and phlegmatic.

LANGUEBEAU
  Murder, murder, murder.   *Within*   245

D'AMVILLE
  Mountains o'erwhelm me – the ghost of old Montferrers
  haunts me.

LANGUEBEAU
  Murder, murder, murder.

D'AMVILLE
  O were my body circumvolved
  Within that cloud, that when the thunder tears   250
  His passage open, it might scatter me
  To nothing in the air!

      Enter LANGUEBEAU SNUFFE *with the* WATCH

LANGUEBEAU   Here you shall find
  The murdered body.
D'AMVILLE   Black Beelzebub
  And all his hell-hounds come to apprehend me?

---

249 *circumvolved* enveloped

---

246 *Mountains o'erwhelm me.* This seems to have been a common cry of
distracted or repentant atheists, deriving perhaps from Hosea 10:8:
'And they shall say to the mountains, Cover us; and to the hills, Fall on
us'; cf. *Dr Faustus*, V.ii, 150–1.
  Dr Faustus was perhaps in Tourneur's mind when he wrote D'Amville's
plea to be consumed in the elements.

LANGUEBEAU

No, my good lord, we come to apprehend   255
The murderer.

D'AMVILLE   The ghost, great Pluto, was
A fool, unfit to be employed in any
Serious business for the state of hell.
Why could not he ha' suffered me to raise
The mountain o' my sins with one as damnable   260
As all the rest, and then ha' tumbled me
To ruin? But apprehend me e'en between
The purpose and the act, before it was
Committed!

WATCH

Is this the murderer? He speaks suspiciously.   265

LANGUEBEAU

No, verily. This is my Lord D'Amville, and his distraction, I
think, grows out of his grief for the loss of a faithful servant,
for surely I take him to be Borachio that is slain.

D'AMVILLE

Ha! Borachio slain? Thou look'st like Snuffe, dost not?

LANGUEBEAU

Yes, in sincerity, my lord.   270

D'AMVILLE

Hark thee – sawest thou not a ghost?

LANGUEBEAU

A ghost? Where, my lord? [*Aside*] I smell a fox.

D'AMVILLE

Here i' th' churchyard.

LANGUEBEAU

Tush, tush, their walking spirits are mere imaginary fables.
There's no such thing in *rerum natura*. Here is a man slain,   275
and with the spirit of consideration I rather think him to be
the murderer got into that disguise than any such fantastic
toy.

D'AMVILLE

My brains begin to put themselves in order. I apprehend thee
now. 'Tis e'en so. – Borachio! – I will search the centre,   280
but I'll find the murderer.

256–64 *The . . . committed* Q gives this speech to Languebeau Snuffe
275 *rerum natura* Snuffe perhaps alludes to Lucretius' *De rerum
      natura,* but it is also possible that he is using the phrase in a
      generalized sense to mean simply 'nature'
280 *centre* of the earth

WATCH
  Here, here, here.
D'AMVILLE
  Stay! Asleep? So soundly? And so sweetly
  Upon death's heads? And in a place so full
  Of fear and horror? Sure there is some other   285
  Happiness within the freedom of the
  Conscience than my knowledge e'er attained to.
  Ho, ho, ho!
CHARLEMONT
  Y' are welcome, uncle. Had you sooner come,
  You had been sooner welcome. I'm the man   290
  You seek. You sha' not need examine me.
D'AMVILLE
  My nephew! And my daughter! O my dear
  Lamented blood, what fate has cast you thus
  Unhappily upon this accident?
CHARLEMONT
  You know, sir, she's as clear as chastity.   295
D'AMVILLE
  As her own chastity. The time, the place,
  All circumstances argue that unclear.
CASTABELLA
  Sir, I confess it, and repentantly
  Will undergo the selfsame punishment
  That justice shall inflict on Charlemont.   300
CHARLEMONT
  Unjustly she betrays her innocence.
WATCH
  But, sir, she's taken with you, and she must
  To prison with you.
D'AMVILLE   There's no remedy,
  Yet were it not my son's bed she abused,
  My land should fly but both should be excused.   305

                                        Exeunt

283–7 *Stay . . . to* as prose Q
305 *fly* be sold

[Act IV, Scene iv]

Enter BELFOREST *and a* SERVANT

BELFOREST
  Is not my wife come in yet?
SERVANT   No, my lord.
BELFOREST
  Methinks she's very affectedly inclined
  To young Sebastian's company o' late,
  But jealousy is such a torment that
  I am afraid to entertain it. Yet   5
  The more I shun by circumstance to meet
  Directly with it, the more ground I find
  To circumvent my apprehension. First
  I know sh' has a perpetual appetite,
  Which being so oft encountered with a man   10
  Of such a bold luxurious freedom as
  Sebastian is, and of so promising
  A body, her own blood, corrupted, will
  Betray her to temptation.

Enter FRESCO *closely*

FRESCO [*Aside*]
  'Precious! I was sent by his lady to see if her lord were in   15
  bed. I should ha' done 't slyly without discovery, and now
  I am blurted upon 'em before I was aware.

                                              Exit
BELFOREST
  Know not you the gentlewoman my wife brought home?
SERVANT
  By sight, my lord. Her man was here but now.
BELFOREST
  Her man? I prithee run and call him quickly.   [*Exit* SERVANT]   20
  This villain, I suspect him ever since
  I found him hid behind the tapestry.

[*Enter* FRESCO *with* SERVANT]

  Fresco! Th'art welcome, Fresco. Leave us.   [*Exit* SERVANT]
  Dost hear, Fresco? Is not my wife at thy mistress's?

  6 *circumstance* going roundabout ways
 11 *luxurious* lecherous
 15 *'Precious* By God's precious blood (or body)
 20–2 *Her . . . tapestry* as prose Q

FRESCO

I know not, my lord.   25

BELFOREST

I prithee tell me, Fresco, we are private, tell me. Is not thy
mistress a good wench?

FRESCO

How means your lordship that? A wench o' the trade?

BELFOREST

Yes faith, Fresco, e'en a wench o' the trade.

FRESCO

O no, my lord. Those falling diseases cause baldness, and my   30
mistress recovers the loss of hair, for she is a periwig
maker.

BELFOREST

And nothing else?

FRESCO

Sells falls and tires and bodies for ladies, or so.

BELFOREST

So, sir, and she helps my lady to falls and bodies now and   35
then, does she not?

FRESCO

At her ladyship's pleasure, my lord.

BELFOREST

Her pleasure, you rogue? You are the pander to her pleasure,
you varlet, are you not? You know the conveyances between
Sebastian and my wife. Tell me the truth, or by this hand   40
I'll nail thy bosom to the earth. Stir not, you dog, but quickly
tell the truth.

FRESCO

O yes!   *Speak[s] like a crier*

BELFOREST

Is not thy mistress a bawd to my wife?

FRESCO

O yes!   45

BELFOREST

And acquainted with her tricks and her plots and her devices?

FRESCO

O yes! If any man, court, city or country, has found my
Lady Levidulcia in bed but my Lord Belforest, it is
Sebastian.

29 *wench o' the trade* bawd
30 *falling diseases* venereal diseases
35 *bodies* bodices

BELFOREST

What, dost thou proclaim it? Dost thou cry it, thou villain? 50

FRESCO

Can you laugh it, my lord? I thought you meant to proclaim yourself cuckold.

Enter the WATCH

BELFOREST

The watch! Met with my wish. I must request th'assistance of your offices.

FRESCO *runs away*

'Sdeath, stay that villain; pursue him. *Exeunt* 55

[Act IV, Scene v]

Enter [LANGUEBEAU] SNUFFE *importuning* SOQUETTE

SOQUETTE

Nay, if you get me any more into the churchyard –

LANGUEBEAU

Why, Soquette, I never got thee there yet.

SOQUETTE

Got me there? No, not with child.

LANGUEBEAU

I promised thee I would not, and I was as good as my word.

SOQUETTE

Yet your word was better then than your deed. But steal up 5
into the little matted chamber o' th' left hand.

LANGUEBEAU

I prithee let it be the right hand; thou left'st me before, and I did not like that.

SOQUETTE

'Precious, quickly – so soon as my mistress shall be in bed I'll come to you. 10

Exit [LANGUEBEAU] SNUFFE

Enter SEBASTIAN, LEVIDULCIA *and* CATAPLASMA

CATAPLASMA

I wonder Fresco stays so long.

SEBASTIAN Mistress

Soquette, a word with you. *Whisper[s]*

LEVIDULCIA If he brings word

My husband is i' bed, I will adventure
One night's liberty to lie abroad. –

11–34 *I . . . faith* as prose Q

My strange affection to this man! 'Tis like   15
That natural sympathy which e'en among
The senseless creatures of the earth commands
A mutual inclination and consent.
For though it seems to be the free effect
Of mine own voluntary love, yet I   20
Can neither restrain it, nor give reason for 't.
But now 'tis done, and in your power it lies
To save my honour or dishonour me.

CATAPLASMA

Enjoy your pleasure, madam, without fear.
I never will betray the trust you have   25
Committed to me, and you wrong yourself
To let consideration of the sin
Molest your conscience. Methinks 'tis unjust
That a reproach should be inflicted on
A woman for offending but with one,   30
When 'tis a light offence in husbands to
Commit with many.

LEVIDULCIA   So it seems to me. –
Why, how now, Sebastian, making love to that gentle-
woman?
How many mistresses ha' you i' faith?

SEBASTIAN

In faith, none, for I think none of 'em are faithful, but   35
otherwise, as many as clean shirts. The love of a woman is
like a mushroom: it grows in one night and will serve
somewhat pleasingly next morning to breakfast, but after-
wards waxes fulsome and unwholesome.

CATAPLASMA

Nay, by Saint Winifred, a woman's love lasts as long as   40
winter fruit.

SEBASTIAN

'Tis true – till new come in, by my experience no longer.

Enter FRESCO *running*

28 ff. Such a defence of women's rights to be unfaithful to their husbands
is not uncommon in the drama of this time. Livia in Middleton's
Women Beware Women is another advocate, arguing that the husband
tastes of many sundry dishes
That we poor wretches never lay our lips to . . .
And if we lick a finger then, sometimes,
We are not to blame; your best cooks use it.
(I.ii, 40 ff.)

FRESCO

    Somebody's doing has undone us, and we are like pay dearly
    for 't.

SEBASTIAN

    Pay dear? For what?   45

FRESCO

    Will 't not be a chargeable reckoning, think you, when here
    are half a dozen fellows coming to call us to account, with
    every man a several bill in his hand that we are not able to
    discharge.   *Knock at the door*

CATAPLASMA

    Passion o' me, what bouncing's that? Madam, withdraw   50
    yourself.

LEVIDULCIA

    Sebastian, if you love me, save my honour.
                         Exeunt [all except SEBASTIAN]

SEBASTIAN

    What violence is this? What seek you? Zounds, you shall
    not pass.

            Enter BELFOREST *and the* WATCH

BELFOREST

    Pursue the strumpet. [*Exeunt* WATCH] Villain, give me way,   55
    Or I will make my passage through thy blood.

SEBASTIAN

    My blood will make it slippery, my lord.
    'Twere better you would take another way.
    You may hap fall else.
          They fight. Both [are] slain. SEBASTIAN *falls first*
          I ha't i' faith.   *Dies*

    While BELFOREST *is staggering,* **enter** LEVIDULCIA

LEVIDULCIA

    O God! My husband! My Sebastian! Husband!   60
    Neither can speak; yet both report my shame.
    Is this the saving of my honour, when
    Their blood runs out in rivers, and my lust
    The fountain whence it flows? Dear husband, let
    Not thy departed spirit be displeased   65
    If with adulterate lips I kiss thy cheek.

48 *bill* halberd, the symbol of office of a constable of the watch
50 *bouncing* knocking
55–85 *Pursue . . . sin* as prose Q
66 *adulterate* that have committed adultery

Here I behold the hatefulness of lust,
Which brings me kneeling to embrace him dead,
Whose body living I did loathe to touch.
Now I can weep. But what can tears do good?   70
When I weep only water, they weep blood.
But could I make an ocean with my tears,
That on the flood this broken vessel of
My body, laden heavy with light lust,
Might suffer shipwreck and so drown my shame,   75
Then weeping were to purpose; but alas,
The sea wants water enough to wash away
The foulness of my name. O, in their wounds
I feel my honour wounded to the death.
Shall I outlive my honour? Must my life   80
Be made the world's example? Since it must,
Then thus in detestation of my deed,
To make th'example move more forcibly
To virtue, thus I seal it with a death
As full of horror as my life of sin.   85

Stabs herself

Enter the WATCH *with* CATAPLASMA, FRESCO, [LANGUEBEAU]
SNUFFE, *and* SOQUETTE

WATCH
  Hold, madam! Lord, what a strange night is this!
LANGUEBEAU
  May not Snuffe be suffered to go out of himself?
WATCH
  Nor you, nor any. All must go with us.
  O with what virtue lust should be withstood,
  Since 'tis a fire quenched seldom without blood.   *Exeunt*   90

Act V, Scene i

Music. A closet discovered. A SERVANT *sleeping with lights and money before him. Enter* D'AMVILLE

D'AMVILLE
  What, sleep'st thou?
SERVANT   No, my lord, nor sleep nor wake,
  But in a slumber troublesome to both.
D'AMVILLE
  Whence comes this gold?
SERVANT   'Tis part of the revenue
  Due to your lordship since your brother's death.
D'AMVILLE
  To bed. Leave me my gold.
SERVANT   And me my rest.   5
  Two things wherewith one man is seldom blest.   *Exit*
D'AMVILLE
  Cease that harsh music. W'are not pleased with it.
                                    He handles the gold
  Here sounds a music whose melodious touch
  Like angels' voices ravishes the sense.
  Behold, thou ignorant astronomer,   10
  Whose wandering speculation seeks among
  The planets for men's fortunes! With amazement
  Behold thine error and be planet-struck.
  These are the stars whose operations make
  The fortunes and the destinies of men.   15
  Yond' lesser eyes of Heaven, like subjects raised
  Into their lofty houses when their prince
  Rides underneath th'ambition of their loves,
  Are mounted only to behold the face
  Of your more rich imperious eminence   20
  With unprevented sight. Unmask, fair queen;
                                    Unpurses the gold
  Vouchsafe their expectations may enjoy
  The gracious favour they admire to see.
  These are the stars, the ministers of fate,
  And man's high wisdom the superior power   25
  To which their forces are subordinate.   *Sleeps*

Enter the GHOST OF MONTFERRERS

21 *unprevented* unobscured

MONTFERRERS
   D'Amville, with all thy wisdom th'art a fool,
   Not like those fools that we term innocents,
   But a most wretched miserable fool,
   Which instantly, to the confusion of   30
   Thy projects, with despair thou shalt behold.   *Exit* GHOST
                                       D'AMVILLE *starts up*

D'AMVILLE
   What foolish dream dares interrupt my rest
   To my confusion? How can that be, since
   My purposes have hitherto been borne
   With prosperous judgement to secure success –   35
   Which nothing lives to dispossess me of
   But apprehended Charlemont, and him
   This brain has made the happy instrument
   To free suspicion, to annihilate
   All interest and title of his own,   40
   To seal up my assurance and confirm
   My absolute possession by the law.
   Thus while the simple, honest worshipper
   Of a fantastic providence groans under
   The burden of neglected misery,   45
   My real wisdom has raised up a state
   That shall eternize my posterity.

       Enter SERVANTS *with the body of* SEBASTIAN

   What's that?
SERVANT   The body of your younger son,
   Slain by the Lord Belforest.
D'AMVILLE   Slain? You lie.
   Sebastian! Speak, Sebastian! H' has lost   50
   His hearing. A physician presently!
   Go, call a surgeon.
ROUSARD   O.   *Within*
D'AMVILLE   What groan was that?
   How does my elder son? The sound came from
   His chamber.
SERVANT   He went sick to bed, my lord.
ROUSARD
   O.   *Within* 55

---

28 *innocents* mentally sub-normal
48–54 *The . . . lord* as prose Q

D'AMVILLE

The cries of mandrakes never touched the ear
With more sad horror than that voice does mine.

Enter a SERVANT *running*

SERVANT

If ever you will see your son alive –

D'AMVILLE

Nature forbid I e'er should see him dead.

A bed drawn forth with ROUSARD

Withdraw the curtains. O how does my son?   60

SERVANT

Methinks he's ready to give up the ghost.

D'AMVILLE

Destruction take thee and thy fatal tongue.
Death! Where's the doctor? Art not thou the face
Of that prodigious apparition stared upon
Me in my dream?   The doctor's come, my lord.   65

SERVANT

Enter DOCTOR

D'AMVILLE

Doctor, behold two patients in whose cure
Thy skill may purchase an eternal fame.
If thou hast any reading in Hippocrates,
Galen, or Avicen, if herbs or drugs
Or minerals have any power to save,   70
Now let thy practice and their sovereign use

62–122 *Destruction . . . soul* as prose Q
71 *sovereign* supreme

---

56 *cries of mandrakes.* The root of the mandrake was said to have human
    shape—hence Donne's impossible command to 'Get with child a man-
    drake roote'—and the plant was believed to scream when pulled from
    the earth, causing anyone who heard the sound to go mad.
59 s.d. *A bed drawn forth.* With this simple stage direction we are to under-
    stand that the scene has shifted slightly, and that we are now in Rou-
    sard's bedroom; the device was a common one—cf. Marlowe's *Massacre
    at Paris*, scene v: '*Enter the* Admiral *in his bed*'.
68–9 *Hippocrates, Galen, or Avicen.* The early medical authorities. Hippo-
    crates (from whom is said to derive the Hippocratic Oath still adminis-
    tered to graduating doctors) was a Greek physician who died in 377
    B.C.; Galen was another Greek, who settled in Rome in the second
    century A.D.; and Avicenna was an Arab doctor (980–1037) whose
    travels were extensive and whose teachings, accordingly, widespread.

Raise thee to wealth and honour.
DOCTOR   If any root
  Of life remains within 'em capable
  Of physic, fear 'em not, my lord.
ROUSARD   O.
D'AMVILLE
  His gasping sighs are like the falling noise   75
  Of some great building when the groundwork breaks.
  On these two pillars stood the stately frame
  And architecture of my lofty house.
  An earthquake shakes 'em; the foundation shrinks.
  Dear Nature, in whose honour I have raised   80
  A work of glory to posterity,
  O bury not the pride of that great action
  Under the fall and ruin of itself.
DOCTOR
  My lord, these bodies are deprived of all
  The radical ability of Nature.   85
  The heat of life is utterly extinguished.
  Nothing remains within the power of man
  That can restore them.
D'AMVILLE   Take this gold; extract
  The spirit of it, and inspire new life
  Into their bodies.
DOCTOR   Nothing can, my lord.   90
D'AMVILLE
  You ha' not yet examined the true state
  And constitution of their bodies. Sure,
  You ha' not. I'll reserve their waters till
  The morning. Questionless, their urines will
  Inform you better.
DOCTOR   Ha, ha, ha.
D'AMVILLE   Dost laugh,   95
  Thou villain? Must my wisdom that has been
  The object of men's admiration now
  Become the subject of thy laughter?
ROUSARD   O.   *Dies*

72–3 *root Of life* essential basis of life

85 *radical ability*. In medieval philosophy, this was the humour or moisture
   which was essential to the life of all plant and animal forms.
88 *gold*. The tincture of gold (*aurum potabile*) was thought to have great
   healing powers; cf. Chaucer, *The Canterbury Tales*: 'For gold in phisik
   is a cordial' (Prologue, l.444).

ALL
  He's dead.
D'AMVILLE   O there expires the date
    Of my posterity. Can Nature be   100
    So simple or malicious to destroy
    The reputation of her proper memory?
    She cannot. Sure there is some power above
    Her that controls her force.
DOCTOR   A power above Nature?
    Doubt you that, my lord? Consider but   105
    Whence man receives his body and his form:
    Not from corruption like some worms and flies,
    But only from the generation of
    A man, for Nature never did bring forth
    A man without a man; nor could the first   110
    Man, being but the passive subject, not
    The active mover, be the maker of
    Himself; so of necessity there must
    Be a superior power to Nature.
D'AMVILLE
    Now to myself I am ridiculous.   115
    Nature, thou art a traitor to my soul.
    Thou hast abused my trust. I will complain
    To a superior court to right my wrong.
    I'll prove thee a forger of false assurances.
    In yond' Star Chamber thou shalt answer it.   120
    Withdraw the bodies. O the sense of death
    Begins to trouble my distracted soul.   *Exeunt*

[Act V, Scene ii]

Enter JUDGES *and* OFFICERS

1 JUDGE
  Bring forth the malefactors to the bar.

Enter CATAPLASMA, SOQUETTE *and* FRESCO

  Are you the gentlewoman in whose house
  The murders were committed?
CATAPLASMA   Yes, my lord.

120 *Star Chamber* the Tudor royal council sitting under the star-
    spangled ceiling of a chamber in the Palace of Westminster as the
    High Court of Justice (and, of course, Heaven)

1 JUDGE
That worthy attribute of gentry which
Your habit draws from ignorant respect   5
Your name deserves not, nor yourself the name
Of woman, since you are the poison that
Infects the honour of all womanhood.

CATAPLASMA
My lord, I am a gentlewoman, yet
I must confess my poverty compels   10
My life to a condition lower than
My birth or breeding.

2 JUDGE   Tush, we know your birth.

1 JUDGE
But under colour to profess the sale
Of tires and toys for gentlewomen's pride,
You draw a frequentation of men's wives   15
To your licentious house, and there abuse
Their husbands.

FRESCO   Good my lord, her rent is great.
The good gentlewoman has no other thing
To live by but her lodgings; so she's forced
To let her fore-rooms out to others, and   20
Herself contented to lie backwards.

2 JUDGE   So.

1 JUDGE
Here is no evidence accuses you
For accessaries to the murder; yet
Since from the spring of lust which you preserved
And nourished ran th'effusion of that blood,   25
Your punishment shall come as near to death
As life can bear it. Law cannot inflict
Too much severity upon the cause
Of such abhorred effects.

2 JUDGE   Receive your sentence.
Your goods, since they were gotten by that means   30
Which brings diseases, shall be turned to th'use

5 *ignorant respect* respect given by those who are ignorant of the
recipient
9–12 *My . . . breeding* as prose Q
17–21 *Good . . . backwards* as prose Q
21 *lie backwards* i.e., in the back bedroom

Of hospitals; you carted through the streets
According to the common shame of strumpets,
Your bodies whipped till with the loss of blood
You faint under the hand of punishment.   35
Then, that the necessary force of want
May not provoke you to your former life,
You shall be set to painful labour, whose
Penurious gains shall only give you food
To hold up nature, mortify your flesh,   40
And make you fit for a repentant end.

ALL

O good my lord!

1 JUDGE   No more; away with 'em.

       Exeunt [CATAPLASMA, SOQUETTE, *and* FRESCO]

       Enter LANGUEBEAU SNUFFE

2 JUDGE

Now, Monsieur Snuffe, a man of your profession
Found in a place of such impiety!

LANGUEBEAU

I grant you the place is full of impurity. So much the more   45
need of instruction and reformation. The purpose that
carried me thither was with the spirit of conversion to purify
their uncleanness, and I hope your lordship will say the law
cannot take hold o' me for that.

1 JUDGE

No, sir, it cannot; but yet give me leave   50
To tell you that I hold your wary answer
Rather premeditated for excuse
Than spoken out of a religious purpose.
Where took you your degrees of scholarship?

LANGUEBEAU

I am no scholar, my lord. To speak the sincere truth, I am   55
Snuffe the tallow-chandler.

2 JUDGE

How comes your habit to be altered thus?

LANGUEBEAU

My Lord Belforest, taking a delight in the cleanness of
my conversation, withdrew me from that unclean life and

43–4 *Now . . . impiety* as prose Q

---

32 *carted.* The usual punishment ('common shame') for whores and
    bawds was that they should be dragged through the streets at the tail of
    a cart and whipped.

put me in a garment fit for his society and my present   60
profession.

1 JUDGE
His lordship did but paint a rotten post,
Or cover foulness fairly. Monsieur Snuffe,
Back to your candle-making. You may give
The world more light with that than either with   65
Instruction or th' example of your life.

LANGUEBEAU
Thus the Snuffe is put out.   *Exit* SNUFFE

Enter D'AMVILLE *distractedly, with the hearses of his two sons
borne after him*

D'AMVILLE
Judgement, judgement!

2 JUDGE   Judgement, my lord, in what?

D'AMVILLE
Your judgements must resolve me in a case.
Bring in the bodies. Nay, I will ha't tried.   70
This is the case, my lord: my providence,
Even in a moment, by the only hurt
Of one, or two, or three at most – and those
Put quickly out o' pain too, mark me; I
Had wisely raised a competent estate   75
To my posterity; and is there not
More wisdom and more charity in that,
Than for your lordship, or your father, or
Your grandsire to prolong the torment and
The rack of rent from age to age upon   80
Your poor penurious tenants, yet perhaps
Without a penny profit to your heir?
Is 't not more wise, more charitable? Speak.

1 JUDGE
He is distracted.

D'AMVILLE   How? Distracted? Then
You ha' no judgement. I can give you sense   85
And solid reason for the very least

68–94 *Judgement . . . that* as prose Q
80 *rack of rent* rackrent was an exorbitant rent, close to the actual
value of the property rented

---

62 *paint a rotten post.* Bullen suggests that this alludes to the custom of
repainting the posts which stood at the doors of a sheriff's house when-
ever a new sheriff came into office.

Distinguishable syllable I speak.
Since my thrift was more charitable, more
Judicious than your grandsire's, why, I would
Fain know why your lordship lives to make   90
A second generation from your father,
And the whole fry of my posterity
Extinguished in a moment, not a brat
Left to succeed me – I would fain know that.

2 JUDGE
Grief for his children's death distempers him.   95

1 JUDGE
My lord, we will resolve you of your question.
In the meantime vouchsafe your place with us.

D'AMVILLE
I am contented, so you will resolve me.   *Ascends*

Enter CHARLEMONT *and* CASTABELLA

2 JUDGE
Now, Monsieur Charlemont, you are accused
Of having murdered one Borachio that   100
Was servant to my Lord D'Amville. How can
You clear yourself? Guilty or not guilty?

CHARLEMONT
Guilty of killing him, but not of murder.
My lords, I have no purpose to desire
Remission for myself.

                   D'AMVILLE *descends to* CHARLEMONT
D'AMVILLE   Uncivil boy,   105
Thou want'st humanity to smile at grief.
Why dost thou cast a cheerful eye upon
The object of my sorrow, my dead sons?

1 JUDGE
O good my lord, let charity forbear
To vex the spirit of a dying man.   110
A cheerful eye upon the face of death
Is the true countenance of a noble mind.
For honour's sake, my lord, molest it not.

D'AMVILLE
Y'are all uncivil. O, is't not enough
That he unjustly hath conspired with Fate   115
To cut off my posterity, for him
To be the heir to my possessions, but

105–8 *Uncivil . . . sons* as prose Q
114–20 *Y'are . . . grief* as prose Q

He must pursue me with his presence, and
In the ostentation of his joy
Laugh in my face and glory in my grief?   120

CHARLEMONT
D'Amville, to show thee with what light respect
I value death and thy insulting pride,
Thus, like a warlike navy on the sea,
Bound for the conquest of some wealthy land,
Passed through the stormy troubles of this life   125
And now arrived upon the armed coast,
In expectation of the victory
Whose honour lies beyond this exigent,
Through mortal danger, with an active spirit,
Thus I aspire to undergo my death.   130
            Leaps up the scaffold. CASTABELLA *leaps after him*

CASTABELLA
And thus I second thy brave enterprise.
Be cheerful, Charlemont. Our lives cut off
In our young prime of years are like green herbs
Wherewith we strew the hearses of our friends,
For as their virtue gathered when th'are green,   135
Before they wither or corrupt, is best,
So we in virtue are the best for death
While yet we have not lived to such an age
That the increasing canker of our sins
Hath spread too far upon us.   140
                                        A boon, my lords;
D'AMVILLE
I beg a boon.
1 JUDGE   What's that, my lord?
D'AMVILLE
His body when 'tis dead
For an anatomy.
2 JUDGE   For what, my lord?
D'AMVILLE
Your understanding still comes short o' mine.   145
I would find out by his anatomy
What thing there is in Nature more exact
Than in the constitution of myself.
Methinks my parts and my dimensions are
As many, as large, as well composed as his,   150
And yet in me the resolution wants

143 *anatomy* dissection
144 *comes* ed. (come Q)
146 *exact* perfect

> To die with that assurance as he does.
> The cause of that in his anatomy
> I would find out.

1 JUDGE   Be patient and you shall.

D'AMVILLE

> I have bethought me of a better way.
> Nephew, we must confer. Sir, I am grown   155
> A wondrous student now o' late. My wit
> Has reached beyond the scope of Nature; yet
> For all my learning I am still to seek
> From whence the peace of conscience should proceed.

CHARLEMONT

> The peace of conscience rises in itself.   160

D'AMVILLE

> Whether it be thy art or nature, I
> Admire thee, Charlemont. Why, thou hast taught
> A woman to be valiant. I will beg
> Thy life. My lords, I beg my nephew's life.
> I'll make thee my physician. Thou shalt read   165
> Philosophy to me. I will find out
> Th'efficient cause of a contented mind;
> But if I cannot profit in 't, then 'tis
> No more, being my physician, but infuse
> A little poison in a potion when   170
> Thou giv'st me physic, unawares to me.
> So I shall steal into my grave without
> The understanding or the fear of death,
> And that's the end I aim at, for the thought
> Of death is a most fearful torment; is't not?   175

2 JUDGE

> Your lordship interrupts the course of law.

1 JUDGE

> Prepare to die.

CHARLEMONT   My resolution's made.

> But ere I die, before this honoured bench,
> With the free voice of a departing soul,
> I here protest this gentlewoman clear   180
> Of all offence the law condemns her for.

CASTABELLA

> I have accused myself. The law wants power

154–9 *I . . . proceed* as prose Q
161–75 *Whether . . . not* as prose Q
167 *efficient cause* a philosophical concept denoting that which makes
   a thing what it is

To clear me. My dear Charlemont, with thee
I will partake of all thy punishments.

CHARLEMONT　　　　　　　　　　　　　　　185
Uncle, for all the wealthy benefits
My death advances you, grant me but this:
Your mediation for the guiltless life
Of Castabella, whom your conscience knows
As justly clear as harmless innocence.

D'AMVILLE　　　　　　　　　　　　　　　190
Freely. My mediation for her life,
And all my interest in the world to boot,
Let her but in exchange possess me of
The resolution that she dies withal.
The price of things is best known in their want.
Had I her courage, so I value it,　　　　　195
The Indies should not buy't out o' my hands.

CHARLEMONT
Give me a glass of water.

D'AMVILLE　　　　　　　　Me, of wine.
This argument of death congeals my blood.
Cold fear, with apprehension of thy end,
Hath frozen up the rivers of my veins.　　　200
　　　　　　　[A SERVANT *gives him*] *a glass of wine*
I must drink wine to warm me and dissolve
The obstruction, or an apoplexy will
Possess me. Why, thou uncharitable knave,
Dost bring me blood to drink? The very glass
Looks pale and trembles at it.

SERVANT　　　　　　　　'Tis your hand, my lord.　205

D'AMVILLE
Canst blame me to be fearful, bearing still
The presence of a murderer about me?

CHARLEMONT
Is this water?

SERVANT
Water, sir.　　　　　　　[*Gives him*] *a glass of water*

CHARLEMONT
Come, thou clear emblem of cool temperance,　210
Be thou my witness that I use no art
To force my courage, nor have need of helps
To raise my spirits, like those weaker men

190–6 *Freely . . . hands* as prose Q
198 *argument* discussion
201–7 *I . . . me* as prose Q

Who mix their blood with wine, and out of that
Adulterate conjunction do beget   215
A bastard valour. Native courage, thanks.
Thou lead'st me soberly to undertake
This great hard work of magnanimity.

D'AMVILLE

Brave Charlemont, at the reflection of
Thy courage my cold fearful blood takes fire,   220
And I begin to emulate thy death.
                    [EXECUTIONER *comes forward*]
Is that thy executioner? My lords,
You wrong the honour of so high a blood
To let him suffer by so base a hand.

JUDGES

He suffers by the form of law, my lord.   225

D'AMVILLE

I will reform it. Down, you shag-haired cur.
The instrument that strikes my nephew's blood
Shall be as noble as his blood. I'll be
Thy executioner myself.

1 JUDGE

Restrain his fury. Good my lord, forbear.   230

D'AMVILLE

I'll butcher out the passage of his soul
That dares attempt to interrupt the blow.

2 JUDGE

My lord, the office will impress a mark
Of scandal and dishonour on your name.

CHARLEMONT

The office fits him; hinder not his hand,   235
But let him crown my resolution with
An unexampled dignity of death.
Strike home. Thus I submit me. [*Makes*] *ready for execution*

CASTABELLA   So do I.
In scorn of death thus hand in hand we die.

D'AMVILLE

I ha' the trick on 't, nephew. You shall see   240
How easily I can put you out of pain. – O.
   As he raises up the axe [he] strikes out his own brains, [and
                 then] staggers off the scaff

218 *magnanimity* greatness of spirit
219–29 *Brave . . . myself* as prose Q
221 *emulate thy death* feel as brave as you in facing death
240–68 *I . . . Castabella* as prose Q

EXECUTIONER
  In lifting up the axe, I think h' has knocked
  His brains out.
D'AMVILLE   What murderer was he
  That lifted up my hand against my head?
1 JUDGE
  None but yourself, my lord.
D'AMVILLE   I thought he was   245
  A murderer that did it.
1 JUDGE   God forbid.
D'AMVILLE
  Forbid? You lie, judge; he commanded it
  To tell thee that man's wisdom is a fool.
  I came to thee for judgement, and thou think'st
  Thyself a wise man. I outreached thy wit   250
  And made thy justice murder's instrument
  In Castabella's death and Charlemont's,
  To crown my murder of Montferrers with
  A safe possession of his wealthy state.
CHARLEMONT   255
  I claim the just advantage of his words.
2 JUDGE
  Descend the scaffold and attend the rest.
D'AMVILLE
  There was the strength of natural understanding.
  But Nature is a fool. There is a power
  Above her that hath overthrown the pride
  Of all my projects and posterity,   250
  For whose surviving blood I had erected
  A proud monument, and struck 'em dead
  Before me, for whose deaths I called to thee
  For judgement. Thou didst want discretion for
  The sentence, but yond' power that struck me knew   265
  The judgement I deserved, and gave it. O,
  The lust of death commits a rape upon me,
  As I would ha' done on Castabella.   *Dies*
1 JUDGE
  Strange is his death and judgement. With the hands
  Of joy and justice I thus set you free.   270
  The power of that eternal providence
  Which overthrew his projects in their pride
  Hath made your griefs the instruments to raise
  Your blessings to a greater height than ever.

CHARLEMONT
    Only to Heaven I attribute the work,   275
    Whose gracious motives made me still forbear
    To be mine own revenger. Now I see
    That *patience is the honest man's revenge.*
1 JUDGE
    Instead of Charlemont that but e'en now
    Stood ready to be dispossessed of all,   280
    I now salute you with more titles, both
    Of wealth and dignity, than you were born to.
    And you, sweet madam, Lady of Belforest,
    You have that title by your father's death.
CASTABELLA
    With all the titles due to me increase   285
    The wealth and honour of my Charlemont,
    Lord of Montferrers, Lord D'Amville, Belforest,
    And for a close to make up all the rest,
                          Embrace[s CHARLEMONT]
    The lord of Castabella. Now at last
    Enjoy the full possession of my love,   290
    As clear and pure as my first chastity.
CHARLEMONT
    The crown of all my blessings! I will tempt
    My stars no longer, nor protract my time
    Of marriage. When those nuptial rites are done,
    I will perform my kinsmen's funerals.   295
1 JUDGE
    The drums and trumpets interchange the sounds
    Of death and triumph for these honoured lives
    Succeeding their deserved tragedies.
CHARLEMONT
    Thus by the work of Heaven the men that thought
    To follow our dead bodies without tears   300
    Are dead themselves, and now we follow theirs.   *Exeunt*

FINIS

Printed in Great Britain by
Whitstable Litho Printers Ltd., Whitstable, Kent